11 Selected Stories Of Munshi Premchand

Renowned Hindi Author

Munshi Premchand

DIAMOND BOOKS

www.diamondbook.in

Publisher : **Diamond Pocket Books (P) Ltd.**
X-30, Okhla Industrial Area, Phase-II
New Delhi-110020

Phone : 011- 40712200
E-mail : sales@dpb.in
Website : www.diamondbook.in

---

11 Selected Stories Of Munshi Premchand

Author : Munshi Premchand

Translated by Surajit Mahalanobis

Publisher's Note

The story is the strongest of all arts of literature. A mirror of such importance it is, in which one can see through the life, in all its shades and silhouettes, in which one can observe all the intrinsic moments of happiness and dejection of man in his interaction with the society, including different streams of actions—all in lively, attractive and soulful traits. To develop it, enormous contributions were made by fiction writers world over. All their crafts, forms, and aesthetics, all their artistic graces are very important in view of evaluation of their techniques.

As for the Hindi Literature, it is an attainment that at the very initial times of its journey, it got a deft painter of human mind like Munshi Premchand. His fictions not only introduced in Hindi, the novel Hindi-Urdu fusion, they also effected the foundation of a new philanthropic heritage of welfare society, while lashing at the hollow considerations of the contemporary socio-economic Indian world, which he depicted while laying down his ideological convictions. However it is the expression of innate strength of Hindi Literature that, notwithstanding heterogeneous onslaughts on its forms and structures, it never allowed itself cut away from the tradition of life depicted by Munshi Premchand, or his noble thought process.

The firmament of Premchand's stories is vast. In view of variety of topics, he, as though, had encompassed the entire sky of humane world into his fold. The renowned critic of Hindi Literature, Dr Goutam Sachdev, had stated of him, while evaluating his fictions and very fittingly substantial a statement that was: "The elements of pre-conceived thoughts guide his fictions. It is an important aspect of Premchand's art of story telling that he would exhibit the actions unfold themselves after he had spread the mat of his pre-conceived ideas. One might ask here, how Premchand developed a story on the mat of a pre-conceived idea? Did he think out his characters, events, and circumstances after having forethought his ideas? Or did he place them before his purviews in advance and thereafter apply his ideas to effect a context? When once he was asked by the editor of a literary monthly from Lahore, Nourangey Khyal, as to how did he use to write his fictions, Premchand had replied: "My fictions are generally based upon some inspiration or experience. I try to create dramatic tinges upon them. I do not write only to tell an event or to narrate any 'recreative happening'. I try to show through my fictions some philosophical or emotional points. As long as I do not get any such base, my pen doesn't get its flow." That statement of Premchand is relevant even today.

Each of Premchand's stories unravels many sides of human mind, many streaks of human's conscience, the evils in some societal practices and heterogeneous angles of economic tortures. All this is done with complete artistry. The "Kafan", "Namak Ka Daroga", "Shatranj Ke Khiladi", "Narak Ka Marg", "Poos Ka Raat", "Panch Parmeshwar", "Do Bailon Ke Katha", "Wasana Ki Karhiyan", "Duniya Ke Sab Se Anmol Ratan", etcetera are there among hundreds of short stories by him which stir the readers' mind even today by means of their variegated layers of thoughts and feelings. They are all the heralds of human glories coming from the pen of a time-tested author. The stories of Munshi, fighting on behalf of the downtrodden of the society, who are suffering from the social and economic agonies, are the strongest assets of our Literature.

Also, in terms of artistry, Premchand's fictions are important. His stories had greatly influenced his contemporaries as much as they still does influence his posterity. In weaving of his plots he consciously applied his crafts which he devised. His fictions came into existence by help of natural human characters, trustworthy events and simple circumstances, and thereafter grew up from these foundations. The very intrinsic nature of his stories, their external formats unfold their entire uniqueness and appeal to the reader's mind. Owing to such special features Premchand's stories are still relevant today, as much as they were five decades ago. The world of his fictions is ever new.

It had been our aspiration that we should present economy-priced books of the immortal Premchand Literature for the palate of enlightened Diamond readers, in attractive get-up. The present edition is only a step towards that goal.

–Narender Kumar Verma
nk@dpb.in

Preface

Rendering *Premchand* (1880—1936) into English is a formidable task. One is immediately confronted by two traits of problems: one, the use of imageries, and two, the implied suggestions for social reforms. The urges well up from within. In the whole gamut of his short stories they emanate from a wavelength which is probably a byproduct off a fusion of physical experiences and historical process. The first is quite discernible. The plot moves straight in romantic overtones with profuse adjectives emphasizing points. For, as was the theme, the novel awareness of people of the time from the English education and the agony from alien domination of the country had stirred the very roots of Indian sentiments. Man was much drawn to his own state of affairs, as though, taking refuge into his ingrown shelters.

What is complex, that is the second problem, is the duty of identifying historical process that worked at the roots of people's mind. Without grasping them one cannot go much far. Truly, Munsi Premchand's protagonists in 'Mansarovar' are often found in the mid-stream of consciousness, often muttering to their own inner soul, while trying to ward off, their mundane challenges in determined bid to attain the happiness ever since unknown to them. This is like mauvaise foi, as Sartre termed when a protagonist is intrigued alike. (Cf. *Being and Nothingness* by Jean Paul Sartre; 1943).

This unknown happiness, however, remains generally unattainable in the end. For, seldom he offers any bold solution.

We may take examples from themes of love in these stories. In normal man-woman love relationship, say—between Sophiya and Vinay, Chakradhar and Manorama, Mani and Indranath, Mangru and Goura, or Keshav and Prema and the likes—love never attains its natural expected end. Neither union nor marriage takes place. Even in the triangles—say between Amarnath and Sakina (*Karmabhumi*) a novel for change, Krishna and Tara (*Vidrohi* or The Rebel), Ivan and Helen (*Kaidee* or The Prisoner) — love fails to reach its desired goal, that is, the romantic union. Unsteadiness in approach to a problem looms large even in Munshi Premchand's stories on socio-political imbroglios, say in the confusion of Chhaukaurhilal of *Tawan* (Recompense).

However, the greatness of Munshi Premchand cannot be minimised by these minor things. His mastery over the plot construction, in emphasising the psyche of his characters, in suggesting the great possibilities, in drawing characters permanently humane for all times to come etcetera are still unsurpassed by any of the latter-day Hindi writers. With similar mastery recorded in Bengali Literature (in Sarat Chandra and, before them to a great extent in Tagore) Munshi Premchand's oeuvre comprises mines of philanthropic traits. The spoken language, conveying what otherwise should be in stream of conscious musings and unspeakable, makes the translation difficult. Adjectives looking similar though, are frequently used to convey streaks of nuances, and they gradually turn to be the things of joy. The sum total is, Munshi Premchand outlives his time.

Transliteration hence is impossible. For the elements which are very essentially Indian and the ethos having roots entrenched in soil of Oriental lands make the assigned job unapproachable. Nascent psyche of people vibed with realism of the existing life, and this surely was hitherto unknown to the worlds outside the original boundaries of India.

On many occasions I had broken the tempo of writing, afraid I would miss the original tenor. Often I dropped working when gone out of wits, abjectly hopeless about my abilities. I think readers would stop denouncing me considering the fact that Munshi Premchand by himself is an age in Hindi Literature, forget about anything else —*chhayavad* or no *chhayavad*.

The first part took almost two years, the second a half, the third is in progress, the others are yet in inept unbecomingness, awaiting precious moods, the tempo of perfection. Alas! How useless I am!

My inner worlds however have undaunted patience. I am grateful to Narender Kumarji, the publishing wizard. He knows how to hold the time. I am thankful to my parents, my wife and my children who constantly offer me succour of courage and understanding silently, days in years out.

–Surajit Mahalanobis

Contents

1. THE MISTRESS OF THE HOUSE
(Swamini)

Shivdas dropped the key of the storeroom in front of his daughter-in-law Rampyari and with tears in his old eyes said: 'Baku, from today onwards charge of this household will rest upon you. God could not relish my happiness, or He won't have snatched away my young son! Somebody however has to do his share of the work. If one plough I have to keep aside unused, subsistence of the household might be stopped. It was of course my bad deeds which is why God has inflicted such an onslaught of punishment onto me, and it is me alone who must accept it upon bowed head. From now onwards I would take charge of the plough which Birju used to work with. For maintenance of the household, for holding-all in preserve who else is here save you? No, don't you cry my child. What God willed has happened, and what He would wish further will again take place. What can you and I do? Now, as long as I'm alive, nobody would dare to cast an angry look upon you. Do not you worry about anything, Birju has left us though, I'm still in control here.'

Rampyari and Ramdulari were two real sisters. Both were married to two real brothers—Mathura and Birju. Both the sisters were living at their in-laws' with the same care and joy as they lived at their parents'. Shivdas was getting pension. All the days hence he would spend in tittle-tattle at his doors. He used to feel delighted at his prosperous family and yoked himself more in religious discussions, but as was the irony of fate, his elder son Birju had fallen ill and today was the fifteenth day that he died.

Having done with the scriptural rites today, Shivdas, like a true karmaveer, once again braced himself up for the struggle for existence. Howsoever agonised he must have been, nobody ever saw tears in his eyes. Today all for a moment as he looked up at his daughter-in-law, his eyes got tearful, but he held his emotion; and then in choked voice began consoling her. Never had he the inkling that he would be required to wipe tears of the widow, who was destined to be the mistress of the household, or at least he would be at all required to do such laborious tasks. That is exactly why he had dropped the key of the store for the entire household. He wanted to suppress the agony of her widowhood under the smugness of domination.

Amused, Rampyari asked: 'How can it be possible dada, that you would do physical labour and I become the mistress of the household? If instead I remain yoked at work I might be able to keep up my heart and soul. In leisurely life I would only bewail and do nothing else.'

Shivdas consoled her: 'My child, nobody has any say upon the providence of God. What would you get from bewailing except fatigue? Scores of things are here on the household to do. Some saints might call on us, some guests might come too, someone must stay at home to attend them.'

His daughter-in-law offered many excuses, but Shivdas didn't accept any of hers.

2

As Rampyari picked up the key after Shivdas went out, she felt a unique sense of pride and responsibility. For a while she even forgot the agony of losing her husband. Her younger sister and the brother-in-law were gone at their works. Shivdas was out. The entire household was too quiet.

At that time, quite self-assured she could open the store. Soon she felt temptation to see what was there inside, what magnificence lay there in it. Never had she gone into it. Whenever somebody was to be given anything, or anything was to be received from somebody, Shivdas used to come and open the room. After that he used to lock the room and keep its key tied with his waist.

Occasionally, Rampyari used to peep through the doors of the room, but nothing was to be visible in the darkness inside. For the entire household that room was magical or mysterious, about which occasional variegated fancies would be taken of. Today Rampyari got an opportunity to open up that mystery to see for herself. She closed the main gate so nobody should see her open the store-room, none would think: why for no necessity she had opened that room? Then with her hands trembling she unlocked it. Her chest was heaving heavily fearing somebody might knock at the gate. As she stepped inside she felt typical yet greater pleasure than that she used to experience while opening her own chest full of jewellery and clothes. There were stored things like gur, sugar, wheat, barley in large earthen pitchers. In one corner were assortment of large utensils, which were used during times of marriages in the household or were given on loan to others. At one niche, there were receipts of rents tagged and lists of transactions. A majestic personage seemed existing there in the room, as if goddess Lakshmi was present visibly. Rampyari remained seated for half an hour in that spell of magnificence and satiated her soul. Every moment a sense of ownership was instilling in her heart a sort of infatuation. When she came out of that room, her personal impressions were all transformed, as it were, someone had cast a spell upon her.

Right at that moment somebody knocked at the gate. Quickly she locked the store-room and opened the gate. She found her neighbour Jhunia standing in wait to ask for a rupee on loan. Rudely Rampyari said: 'Not a farthing is there at home *jiji*. All the money we had, were spent off in the scriptural rites.'

Jhunia got puzzled. It was hard to believe that at the Chaudhuris' there, was not even a single penny available at that hour. He who transacted in hundreds could not have spent off all the money in scriptural rites. Had Shivdas given the excuse she would not have been astonished. But Pyari was popular in the village for her candid nature. Often she gave her neighbours their desired things slinking away from Shivdas' notice. Only yesterday she gave Janki one seer of milk. She even gave others her ornaments on loan. At the coming of such an open-handed bahu at Shivdas' household villagers considered a stroke of luck.

Surprised Jhunia replied: 'Don't say such thing *jiji*, I've come to you as I'm in a crisis or, you know such is not my habit. I have to pay off an arrear of one rupee. A footman is shouting at my doors. If you help me with the rupee, then somehow the trouble will be averted. I'll come to return that on the eighth day from today. There is no other house in the village from where I might ask for it.'

Pyari did not budge an inch. Soon as she left, Pyari began arranging to cook evening meals. Earlier, picking up rice and pulses seemed to her an immense job, going to the kitchen was no less than getting impaled. For sometimes, the two sisters used to get engaged in arguments over the job, and consequently as Shivdas would interfere asking: 'Well, won't there be any cooking today, one of the two would get up only to half-cook coarse foodstuff which were fit for cattle feeding only'. But today Pyari was yoked in arrangements for cooking with all her hearts and efforts. For she was now the mistress of the household.

Presently she came out and saw hugc garbage dumped outside. 'The *burrahao* only idled away his times all days. He did not even feel it necessary that he should at least sweep the place. Well, cannot he do even this much? The gate look shining as much to please one who looks at it. Not that one should feel like vomitting at its sight. If I tell him now, he might flare up. Eh well, well, why Munni is standing aloof from the manger?'

She came close to Munni and looked down into the manger. Stink was coming out from it. 'Right; it appears, for months water has not been changed. Ah, the cow won't survive like this. Well, well, you have done your fill, so your duty is over? Well then, what else should he have with others to do? But yes of course, everybody likes milk… There dada is smoking from a *chelum*, at the doorstep. Alas, that too worth of three *kouris* only. Whereas the *burrhao* would manage to eat as much as one and a-half seers alright, but if he is yoked in jobs he would feel lost. Let him report today. I'm going to take him to ask as to why he did not change water in the trough? And if he agrees to remain in the service after that he might, or he must quit. Labourers would be found here many. Such people flock all around for jobs.'

At least she could not stand it any longer. She picked up a pitcher.

Shivdas called out for her: 'What will you do with water, bahu? Water is there in it already?'

Pyari replied: 'Water in the manger has got polluted. Munni doesn't put her mouth in the chaff. Can't you see she is standing a *kos* away from it?'

Shivdas smiled touchingly and came forward to take the pitcher from his bahu's hand.

3

Several months passed. Soon as the household came under Pyari's charge spring seemed to have arrived there. Wherever you saw, inside or outside, imprints of some efficient controller's skilful judgment and decent taste would be marked. Pyari screwed up the domestic machine in such a fashion that all its parts were functioning flawlessly. Meals were now of better quality and were served in time. Milk was more in quantity, so was ghee and the workload. Pyari herself won't take rest, nor would she let others take more than required. Plentitude was in the household in such degree that whatever one asked for used to be available within the household itself. From men to animals all looked healthy. Picture of the household was no longer like earlier days when some would move around in tattered clothes or some would be feverishly after ornaments. Well, yes, if anybody ever looked Sickly, care-torn and in shabby outfit, it was the bahu Pyari only; even then the entire family was jealous of her. So much that even the old man Shivdas would take ill of her at times. Nobody relished the practice of getting up at an hour before the dawn. All would shirk off from doing manual labour. Despite all this, all knew it well that without Pyari the household would not have run. Let alone other things even between the two real sisters feeling of oneness was no longer like before.

It was early in the morning Dulari came with her bangles and threw them before Pyari. Petulantly she said: 'Take these two and lock them inside the store.'

Pyari picked the bangles up and replied in her soft voice: 'I've told you already, let me get some spared cash, I'll get it made. These are not yet so worn out that today itself they be put off and thrown away.'

Dulari had come ready to quarrel. She replied: 'Why the spared money would at all come at your hand and why would my bangles be at all made? You only enjoy in saving each and every farthing. Tell no?'

Pyari answered with a smile: 'If I save by each and every opportunity that is for you only. Who do I have after me, that I would save to become most well-off? My *anant* has crumbled down long ago.'

Dulari: You may not eat enough or wear expensive but you acquire reputation alright. And what else is here save eating good and wearing well? I do not have any concern with your accounts, my bangles you must ask today to be made.'

Imbibed with ingenuous fun she asked: 'If I do not have the money, how then would I get it made?'

Dulari replied insolently: 'I don't have anything to do with that. I want my bangles only.'

Like this, folks at the household would heap reproaches onto Pyari as and when they found their chances and the poor woman used to bear everybody's blustering with smiles. It was the duty of the mistress of the house that she must bear with all swaggerings but would speak only wherein lay the family's welfare. Swaggerings, taunts, threats—none has any effect on the shield of authority. Besides her sense of authority generally got clearer after such reactions. She was the conductor of the household. All in the family used to tell her their heart-felt woes but whatever she decided to do only that would be done. And that was enough for her pleasure.

Pyari was commended by the entire village. Even at that young age she was the controlling figure for all the families in the village. Had she had desired she could have married, so to lead an easy life. Instead, she sacrificed herself for this family. Never would she speak to anybody happily, as if she had undergone metamorphosis.

After a few days Dulari's bangles came well-made. For this only Pyari repeatedly called on the goldsmith's.

It was dark already. Dulari and Mathura returned from the mart. Pyari offered the bangles to Dulari. Dulari was instantly delighted. Promptly she put the bangles on and ran to the *barautthe* to show Mathura the bangles. Hiding herself behind the doors of the *barautthe,* Pyari witnessed the scene in longful eyes. Her eyes became full of tears as well. Dulari was only three years younger than her. Yet what a difference was there between the two. The scene almost stuck to her eyes, the ingenuous joy of the couple, their loving embrace, their charmed posture—Pyari gazed at them intently, so much that the two disappeared from her eyes and in the misty light of the lamp the frolicsome scenes of her own past began appearing time and again in many new colours.

Suddenly Shivdas called out for her: '*Barhi bahu,* give me a pice. I would send for tobacco.'

Pyari's stance broken.... Wiping her tears she went in to fetch coin from the store-room.

4

Pyari's ornaments were now being liquidated by her own hands. One by one. She wanted to show, 'my household must look the most prosperous in the village, and of course for such ambition value has to be paid. Sometimes for the repair of the house, sometimes for buying a cow or the bulls, sometimes for expenses of relatives or sometimes for medical treatment money was required, therefore even after much adjustments and readjustments when both ends won't be met, then she would pawn some of her own ornaments to raise the money. And once the ornaments were out they were never retrieved. If she had so desired, many of such expenses would have been avoided, but here it was the prestige involved, so she used to spend freely. If one gets humiliated in stature in the village, what else remain then? People would name only her. Dulari also had ornaments. One-two items were with Mathura too. But Pyari would never touch theirs. It was their days to enjoy. Why must they get entangled in such fuss?

When a son was born to Dulari, Pyari offered to celebrate his birth in great pomp.

Shivdas objected to this: 'What's the use? When by the grace of the Almighty he will grow up enough to be betrothed, you do it at that time in pomp and show.'

But why Pyari's enthused heart could be contained? She replied: 'What are you telling *dada?* If birth of the first child is not celebrated in pomp and show then which else will be the occasion for it? My heart is not consoled at least. This apart what the world around would say? Such great cries with so little wool? I won't solicit anything from you. Everything I'd organise by myself.'

'It would be accounted for your ornaments only what else?' said Shivdas. 'One day even a thread will not be left; if you go on like this. How many times had I persuaded you that nobody actually can be owned—be it a son, a brother, or a sister-in-law. If you save some of your resources with you, then all will look for you. Or none would even talk straight to you.'

Pyari made such a face as if she had heard similar evil talks several times. Thereafter she said: 'If one's own people do not look after him, even then they remain his own. My righteousness remains with me, his with himself. Would I carry my resources piled on me when I would die?'

The birth ceremony was celebrated in pomp. On the twelfth day entire community were feasted. People left after sumptuous meals; tired to her core from day-long labour Pyari spread floor-mat on the courtyard to relax herself. Her eyes blinked to a nap, just then Mathura entered the house. He was curious to see his new-born child. Dulari had cleared out of *soura-griha.* She had become lean from childbirth, her face too had gone charmless, yet a glow of health was spread on her countenance today. The pride and ecstasy of motherhood had infused life into her eyes. The restraints during the post-natal period and the nutritious feeding had made her body well up. Soon as she saw her in the courtyard, Mathura came closer, for once looked aside Pyari to make sure she was asleep, and then took up the child into his lap and caressed it.

Alerted by the sound, Pyari opened her eyes: but she pretended sleeping and with her half-opened eyes she began witnessing such ecstatic game. In turn, the father and the mother was planting kisses at the son embracing and getting lost at staring at him. What a heavenly pleasure was it, for them. For a moment Pyari's thirsty yearning suppressed the mistress in herself. Like a bridled close-bound horse, laden with burden, tormented by flog of the bawling rider, breathless by constant riding, pricks up its ears at whinnying, and instantly forgetting the situation replies with a suppressed note of whinny, something alike happened to Pyari. Her motherhood which was concealed in her cage, mute and effortless, as if suddenly got awakened by the chirping of motherhood close to herself and was flipping its wings anxious to come out of that cage of thoughts.

Mathura said: 'This is my son.'

Dulari clung the child to her lap to say: 'Oh yes why not! It's you who carried in the womb for nine months? Affliction was caused to me and you would jump out to claim ownership owing to fatherhood?'

Mathura: 'If he is not my son why then would he has my countenance. In his lineament and looks does he not resemble me only?'

Dulari: 'How does that matter? The seeds come from the traders, but the farm belongs to the farmer only. The crop goes to the farmer only and not to the traders.'

Mathura: 'Well, well, nobody would be able to win over you in argument. If he turns out to become my son, I would relax at my doors smoking pleasantly from hookah.'

Dulari: 'My son would read and write, earn some prestigious recognition. He won't drag his feet every day behind the oxen. I'm to ask the mistress so that tomorrow orders be given to get a cradle made.'

Mathura: 'From now onwards do not get up very early in the morning and also do not work rigorously.'

Dulari: 'Well, would this Maharani allow me live then?'

Mathura: 'I pity the poor lady. Who she has for herself?' She only dies for all of us. If bhaiya had been alive today she would have been a mother of two or three children.'

Emotion surged up through her throat so much that for suppressing tears her body began trembling. The deprived life of Pyari appeared to her desert-like, in dry sand of which she was making fruitless efforts to grow a lush green garden.

Suddenly Shivdas came in to say: *'Barhi Bahu,* have you gone asleep? The bandsmen have not yet receive their *parose,* what should I tell them?'

5

After some days Shivdas died too. On the other hand two more children were born to Dulari. Even she mostly remained busy in rearing up the children. Responsibility of ploughing fell entirely on the labourers. Mathura was good as a cultivator but not as a supervisor. Never had he any opportunity to take works from people individually. At first he was working under supervision of his elder brother. Later he worked under guidance of his father. He did not know the basics of cultivation. The workers who stayed with him were efficient but in sycophancy only. So Pyari was duty-bound to make rounds at the plough thrice or four times a day. Just for the name sake she was still the mistress of everything, but in reality she was maid-servant of the household. Even the labourers usually frowned at her. The footman of the zamindar would also bluster upon her only. She had cut into her own fooding; the boys were to be given something to eat every time they would ask for. Dulari was mother of sons, she too would need full diet. Mathura was the boss of the family, who could deprive him of his right? Why then, the labourers must have to do any concession hence? The entire compensation would therefore have to be made up by Pyari. She was the lone extra thing in the family who even if ate half a meal every day none would be affected by that. At thirty her hairs turned gray, her waist inclined, eyesight weak, yet she was satisfied. The vanity of becoming the mistress of the household had worked as a balm over these lesions.

One day Mathura said: Bhabhi, I feel like going to some other land now. Here even our earnings have not been increased as yet. Somehow we manage to earn our bread only for ourselves. That too after painstaking labour. Some folks have arrived here from to the east. They say one gets jobs there at wages like two-three rupees a day. If I can stay even for four-five years there we might get rich. We too are parents now. We're required to do something for our children's future.'

Dulari supported him: 'If we can save some resources, we might be able to educate our sons. We have already spent off our lives anyhow, but these boys have to be groomed up well, civilised and good mannered.'

With a proposal such as that Pyari was surprised. She only kept on staring at them. 'Never before such talks were held. How could they be in such ardent desire? Perhaps it's owing to me that they thought out such a thing!' She doubted in herself.

She replied: 'I would never allow you to go but the rest depends upon what you wish. As for educating the boys there runs a *madarsa* here too. Besides, do all days remain as these always? If for two-three years farming run successfully, then all would be set right.'

Mathura: 'We have spent such long period in the farming, yet nothing came out to be called a success. What else is there now likely to happen? Days would pass away like before while our desire would continue to remain unfulfilled. Besides, my strength is gradually waning, who else is there in the family to handle the farming? I don't want to spoil lives of these sons by yoking them constantly in the harness.'

With tears in her eyes Pyari replied: 'Dear brother, as long as some provision is here at home one should not run after those outside. If you have any hitch in your mind regarding me then, take the charge of the household yourself, run it, and just throw a fragment for me to live on. I'll be happy with that.'

In a voice softened by compassion, Mathura answered: 'Bhabhi, why do you utter such words? It's but for your managing that the household could run thus far, or it would have been ruined completely. You have exhausted yourself and your health both for the sake of this family only. I'm not blind! I can understand everything. You should rather permit us to leave. If God so desires, once again our family would pull along together. We would send you expenses regularly.'

Pyari argued: 'If such is your resolve, then both of you go. Leave the children here. Where would you move around with them clung together?'

Dulari: 'How that could be possible sister? Here in rural atmosphere how the children would study? He too would not feel good to himself without them. Frequently would he rush for home, and all his earnings would vanish in fares. This apart, his own expenses at a different place would be so much that entire family might be able to live with that amount, in comforts.'

Pyari replied: 'What then I should do here having been left behind? Take me also along with you.'

Dulari was not in a mind to take her along. She wanted to enjoy life for some days all by her own, if even at the other place same bonds persist like they do here, what was the use in going away at all! She argued: 'Sister, if you could be taken along what could be the better condition, but then entire works would be abandoned to ruin here. At least you will be able to continue to look after something.'

One day before their departure Rampyari woke up for the whole night. To cook for them *halua* and *puri*. Eversince she had entered this household even for once she never had a moment to stay alone. Two real sisters stayed together always. Today having foreseen that terrible moment ensuing Pyari's heart was getting sunk. As she marked Mathura looking happy, the children also had even forgotten to take their food over the zeal for the travel, she too wanted to remain carefree alike, crushing under her feet all the feelings and compassion she had for them, all the dotage and affection. But the nutrients living on which this affection had grown and bloomed all these long years—having witnessed the same being pushed away aside, she could not stop getting annoyed. Dulari was seated in such confidence as if she was going to visit a fair. The eagerness to view novel things, the yearning to move around the new world had rendered her inactive. The responsibility to organise everything hence had fallen on Pyari's head. Have all the clothes arrived from the washerman's or not? Which of the utensils must go into their baggage? How much they must require for their travel—everything. One of the children was almost getting cold, another had diarrhoea for a few days; grinding and pounding herbs for them and many other works kept her busy. Without even being a mother of children she was more efficient in rearing up the kids than Dulari herself. 'Look, don't beat the children much. They become adamant and shameless if thrashed. With children even the adult should become childlike. Sometimes one should play with them, sometimes make funs with them. If you want that you would lay in comfort and the children also should sit silently without thrusting out their hands and feet then remember that it would never happen. Children are vivacious by nature. Keep them engaged in some works. That is much better than giving them half-a-penny toys or thousands of browbeating'. Dulari paid quite unmindful heeds at her suggestions, as if some crazy person was prattling.

The day of departure was the day of test for Pyari. It occurred to her that she should run away from there somewhere else, so that she would not have to witness the scene. Alas, another minute and the house would become desolate. From onwards, for all the days she would be left in the house to herself only. At whom would she make jokes? Whom she should speak to? Her heart shivered at the very thoughts. As the time was approaching, her instinct was getting laxed. Now she would get lost to her thoughts while doing something, and then would she be found staring at something else, and lost again. When she would find some intermittent leisures she was found hurrying aside into privacy to shed quiet tears. She was also consoling herself with talks like 'had they been mine own could they be able to go like this?' or, 'ours is relation of agreement, is there any compulsion of anything on any side?', and 'you do whatever for others, they are never yours own; mix up water as much you like in oil even then they would remain separated.'

The children were moving around majestically clad in new dresses. Pyari was trying to hold them close to herself, to caress, but they were jerking themselves free with countenance about to try. How could she possibly know that given such occasion quite often one's own children become rude. By ten o'clock the bullock-cart arrived at the gate. The children rushed onto it at the first instant. Many males-females came up to see them off. Pyari felt their arrival at that hour itself as bad. She wanted to take Dulari aside in privacy and weep: wanted to tell Mathura with folded hands 'keep on inquiring of my welfare, who else do I have in this world save you?'—but in such crowded din she never found any chance to tell them these. Both Dulari and Mathura climbed up onto the cart and Pyari was left standing at the gate weeping to herself. She was nonplussed so much that she even lost her common urge of sending them off upto the outer of the village.

6

For a few days Pyari lay like swooned. She neither came out of her room nor lighted the hearth, nor she washed her hands and face. The peasants employed there came time and again to say: 'Malkin, please get up. Get fresh, take some food and drink water. How long would you lay down like this?' Women from the village too came to console her alike, but in their words streak of jealousy seemed to her to have been concealed.

From Jokhu's voice of course resounded genuine sympathy for her. Jokhu was a truant, garrulous and addicted fellow. Pyari was in the habit of scolding him always. Once or twice she had even sacked him, but on Mathura's persuasion she had re-employed him again. Even today having heard Jokhu's sympathetic words Pyari would have reacted irritated: 'Why he didn't go to his job? Why is he here waiting on me?' But she did not feel like snubbing him off. At this hour she was hungry of sympathies. Even if the fruits comes from a tree having thorns should that be left aside?

Slowly degree of her resentment became lower. Life started functioning like earlier. The responsibility of entire farming now vested upon her. People suggested: 'Break away one plough and dispose off the farms.' But the vanity of Pyari would not let her accept her own defeat by doing that. Everything ran as before. On the other hand as Mathura never sent her any letter, her self-esteem got further kicked up. 'He thinks I'm awaiting for his shelters. Well, I've enough capability here to feed him too. I would not have got any treasure if he had written to me. If he does not have any concerns about me, well then why must I care for him.'

At home, there was not much work, Pyari began getting whole day yoked in farming. She had sowed musk-melons. That was grown up aplenty, and were sold fast. Earlier, the entire milk was consumed in the family, now the surplus was being sold off. Even in Pyari's attitude novel change came in.

She again began to wear clean clothes, even she was not much indifferent in making herself up. She also developed likings for ornaments. Soon as some spared money she got, she retrieved her mortgaged ornaments, and also began to take balanced diet. Earlier, the sea would soon get empty itself after getting all the fields irrigated. Now the outlets for draining out the water were all closed. Water now remained accumulated in the sea and thin waves came therein enough to be viewed. There also were lotuses bloomed.

One day as Jokhu returned from the fields it was dark. Pyari inquired of him: 'What have you been doing there since long?' Jokhu replied: 'There were only four beds in the fields left for watering. I thought if I could carry on with ten more *mots* somehow, there would not be any worry for tomorrow. Why not do that?'

These days Jokhu was working with all his heart at his job. As long as his master was there overseeing him perform, he did all dilly dallyings. Now everything bestowed upon him, as well. Pyari could not afford to stay all the day at the fields. Sense of responsibility therefore was instilled in him.

Pyari put a *lota* full of water before him and said: 'Alright, now wash your hands and face. A man should be able to work keeping cares about his own health. After all nothing comes out from getting panicky and confused. Tilling could be done even tomorrow if it was difficult today. Why? Was there the hurry?'

Jokhu thought Pyari was getting annoyed. He had worked for some achievement which his intelligence could let him and hoped to be praised for that. Instead he faced adverse comments. Irritated at that he replied: '*Malkin,* you are treading both ways—right and left. Why do you jump into matters which you do not know properly? For tomorrow entire sugarcane field is lying dry there to be watered. Today I got the well for use after long wait. Had I waited for the morning tomorrow somebody else would have created obstruction. In that case we had to look for the eighth day for our next turn. By that time the entire sugarcane would have been spoiled.'

Pyari laughed at his ingenuity and said: 'O you crazy, I'm not accusing you! I just said you should work only having taken care for yourself. Suppose you fall ill, you would face losses instead of gaining.'

Jokhu: 'Who would fall ill? Me? For last twenty years I never once had even headache. Well of course I do not know what might happen in future. If you ask me I can work throughout the night.'

Pyari: 'How do I know that? Every other day you would sit down skipping your duties and when asked you had replied like—'There was fever, or had pain in your stomach'.

Blushed, Jokhu said: 'That was during those days when masters wanted to exploit me at job. Now I understand everything hangs on me. If I don't perform, whole thing would be ruined.'

Pyari: 'Why? Don't I look after that?'

Jokhu: 'Ah, the best you do only is visit those twice a day. You would not be able to sit there for the whole day.'

His artless demeanour impressed Pyari outright. She said: 'So now at this hour of the evening you would go to fire your hearth. Why don't you marry someone?'

Jokhu replied while washing his face: You too speak quite funny, *malkin.* I cannot even afford to meet my basic needs, and to get married to someone? For half a-day itself I consume one and a-quarter of foodstuff. Full one and a-quarter of seer, mind it! For both time meals I need two full seers, do you know?'

Pyari: 'Okay, you take your meal at my place tonight. Let me see for myself, exactly how much you eat.'

Amused Jokhu replied: 'Oh no, *malkin.* You will get tired while cooking for me. But yes, if you make two rotis of half a seer each, then I might eat that gladly. In fact I do the same. Just

I knead the flour and prepare two large thick pancakes and bake them on the fire made from cow-dung cakes. Then I eat them along with butter-milk sometimes or with salt or onions and lay down asleep.'

Pyari: 'I'll feed you today with light thin pancakes.'

Jokhu: 'Then the whole night would be spent in eating only.'

Pyari: 'Now stop chattering, come along quickly, be seated.'

Jokhu: 'Let me go for a while to give fodder to the cattle, first, thereafter I'm coming to sit down for food.'

7

There ensued banterings between Jokhu and Pyari.

Pyari said: 'I tell you, there is no need of sowing the paddy. If there is incessant downpour the field would go under the rainwater. If again the rain stops the field might get dried up. Jowar, millet, hemp, arhar—all are there, of course, why must there be rice too?'

While balancing a large mattock on his shoulder, Jokhu said: 'If all would be able to get their crops, then mine too would grow. If others' fields go under water, then mine too would go under water. Why should I fall behind others? During father's time, only five-bigha area was used for sowing and nothing more than that. Birju bhaiya added one-two bighas more to that. Mathura also added something more every year. Why then I am the inferior to all? I won't sow in area less than five bighas.'

'At that time two young people were there to work.'

'I also eat equal to both of them, why won't I work equal to both of them?'

'Oh, you funny lier. You had been boasting that you eat two seers of food, four seers of food—but you failed just after half a seer at it.'

'Weight one day, you would know of it then.'

'I've already weighed. You a boastful eater, eh? Now, don't sow the paddy, I tell you. Hired peasants would be available, otherwise alone you'd have to be troubled with the ploughs'.

Pyari took away the mattock from his shoulder and said: 'Whole day upto the fall of night you would spend in the pool, whereas I would be fed up left alone in the house.'

Jokhu did not know why one would get fed up at all. If there is no work then people should lie down and sleep? Why to get fed up? He answered: 'If you get fed up alone, then go to sleep. If I stay home then you would get be more fed up. And if I stay idle then I would feel like eating something time and again? Well, here time is being wasted just in fun, whereas it is going to be cloudy.'

Compromising, Pyari said: 'Alright, go to work from tomorrow, come, sit here, relax for today.'

It appeared Jokhu got bounded when he said: 'Okay here I get seated. Now tell me what you intended to tell.'

Pyari replied making fun of him: 'What to say, I'm asking you, why don't you get married? I die working in loneliness. After your marriage, atleast from one I would become two.'

Jokhu blushed and said: 'Yet again you have raised that useless talks *malkin.* To whom should I get married here? And what should I do with the meherian, who might pester me of ornaments?'

Pyari: 'You have spoken out a tough condition, then. Where will you get such a woman who will not even ask for ornaments?'

Jokhu: 'I don't say that she should not ask for ornaments. Yet she should not pester me for that. You never were insistent for ornaments: instead, you spent for others all the ornaments you had.'

Light colours glowed in Pyari's cheeks. She asked: 'Alright, what else is your expectation?'

Jokhu: 'If I start telling these, you might get angry.'

A streak of blush reflected in Pyari's eyes. She replied: 'If you talk things to be angry with, then I definitely would be angry.'

Jokhu: 'Then 1 would not talk.'

Pyari pushed him at his back and said: 'How come, you would not tell? I'll make you talk.'

Jokhu: 'Well, I want that she should be like you—such resolved, as much skilled in talks, such good at cooking and smiling as are you. That's it, if I get such a woman, I might marry, or I should hang on like I'm doing.'

Pyari's face wore on red with blush. Drifting backwards she said: 'You are very naughty! You have said everything posing fun.'

❐

2. THE WELL OF THE THAKUR
(Thakur Ka Kuan)

As Jokhu put his mouth into the *lota,* stink came out from the water in it. He inquired from Gangi: 'What kind of water is this? Its foul smell makes it impossible for drinking. My throat is getting parched and you gave me polluted water to drink?'

Every day in the evening Gangi collected water enough for use in the household. The well was there at a distance, frequenting where was troublesome. Yesterday when she had fetched the water it did not have any stink at all. How could it get fetid today? She put her nose into the *lota;* true, there was the foul smell. Some animal must have fallen into the well and died; but now where from one should get clean water?

Who'll allow her to climb upon the raised circular curb of the well at the Thakurs'? People would rebuke her away right from the distance. The well at the Sahus' however was at the extreme end of the village even then who'll allow her fetch water from there too? There was no other well in the village.

For quite some days Jokhu was ill. Presently he kept lying down for a while suppressing his thirst, then said: 'I cannot stand it any longer, you better give me that, let me drink some from this very water by withholding my breath.'

Gangi did not give him that. His illness might aggravate by drinking polluted water, that much she was aware of; but she did not know that if boiled, the pollution in water lessens. She replied: 'How will you drink this? Who knows what kind of animal had fallen and dead in it? Let me fetch some water from another well.'

Jokhu looked at her in surprise: 'From where will you bring different water?'

—'There are two wells after all—one belongs to the Thakurs and the other to the Sahus. Won't they allow me collect a *lota* full of water?'

—'Yes, you would only return with your hands and legs broken, nothing would happen less than that. Keep seated there without making any fuss. Or, if you go there the god-like Brahmins would bless you with curses, the Thakur would strike you with a lathi, and Sahuji would usurp five other things for giving one. Who appreciates miseries of the poor? We might even die yet none of them would come to our doorstep even to peep through. To become a pall-bearer, if we die, is a far-cry. Well, would such people allow you to collect water from their well?'

There was only bitter truth in those words. Gangi could not put up an answer; yet she did not give him that foul smelling water to drink.

2

It was nine at night. The labour folks had all gone to bed tired out, though at the doorway of Thakurs ten to five of the working people were assembled and gossiping carefree. Gone were the days for battle-field heroism, nor there were any scope for it. They were gossiping on legal battles. How cleverly the Thakur had bribed the police station-incharge and got away with the particular case unscathed. How intelligently he fished out the copy of a remarkable case. Nazir and Mohtimim all were emphatic that collecting the copy was not at all possible. Some would have asked fifty rupees for it, some hundred. But here without paying a farthing to anybody he removed the copy of the case. Well one should know the method of doing a job.

Right at that hour Gangi reached the well for dragging out water.

The dimming light from a lamp had fallen on the curb of the well. Behind the raised circular curb around the well she lay secretively in wait for the opportune moment. The entire village drank water from that well. There was no prohibition for anybody, only they—the luckless folks—could not fetch water from it.

The imaginary revolting group of Gangi began launching attacks on these customary restrictions and difficulties. Why are we considered low-born and why are they called high-born? Is it because these people put on thread round their necks? Whosoever are here each one of them is the choicest evil-doer. Stealing they do, deceit and fraud they plot, false litigation they impose. Even on the other day this very Thakur had stolen a lamb that belonged to the Garariyas, killed it and eaten. In the households of these pandits gambling takes place throughout all the months of a year. The very Sahuji mixes oil in ghee before selling it. They all take labour from people but while paying the wages they drag cold feet. On which grounds are they superior to us? Yes, in terms of vaunting of course they are superior to us. We do not go walking down lanes after lanes bragging: 'We are high-born—the high-born'. If ever I happen to come inside the village, they look at me with revengeful concern, as if they're tormenting in envy! Yet they would boast 'We're the higher-ups'.

There were sounds as of someone's footsteps. Gangi's heart began palpitating. Disaster would fall on her if she was spotted. Not one step even would fall flat carelessly. She picked up the rope and pitcher and hurried back in stooped posture. Soundlessly she took cover into the darkened shadow of a tree. Who knew when would these people have perilous mercy on whom. They had beaten poor Mahangu so severely that for months he had been spitting blood. Only because he had refused to work without remuneration. And after all this, these people pose to become superiors?

Two women had come to the well to fetch water. They were talking: 'We were about to sit for our meals, when came his order to fetch fresh water from the well. There is no money for spared pitchers.'

—'The males seem to feel envious whenever they see us seated in comforts.'

—'Yes. They'd never feel, like picking up the pitcher and fetch water themselves. Instead they would only command —bring fresh water —as if we are maid servants.

—'What else you think you are? Don't you get bread and clothings? Also you manage to collect ten-five bucks by scrambling. How else one becomes a maid-servant otherwise?'

—'Don't make me ashamed, *didi.* My heart remains pining for short rest every day which I can't. Had I had worked so much at others household, I would have lived much more comfortably. Top of it, that fellow would have felt obliged too. Here at this household, you might die working for them hard, yet none would be pleased.'

As they left having collected the water, Gangi came out of the shadow of the tree and walked close to the curb of the well. Her carelessness was gone by then. Even the Thakur was preparing to go inside the courtyard to sleep as he was seen closing the door. For a moment Gangi took a sigh of relief. Somehow her field was clear now. The prince who once upon a time had gone to steal away the nectar, might not have taken such care or gone with such keenness of understanding, as she acted with. With tiptoes.

Gangi climbed up the curb. Never before had she relished such a victory.

She fastened up the pitcher with a loop of the rope. With alert eyes she looked around, left and right, as if a soldier was busy drilling a hole in enemy's fortress. If at this moment she was caught, then for her there was not an iota of hope for pardon or favour. At last recalling her gods for protection she held her heart and drowned the pitcher into well.

The pitcher dipped into the water, very silently. Not wee bit of sound came out from there. Very quickly in several free-handed lifts Gangi pulled up the pitcher. It came up to the level of the well-mouth. Even a big strong hefty-sturdy man could not have pulled the pitcher up faster as did she.

With a stoop Gangi held the pitcher, put it on the curb and all of that sudden moment Thakur Sahib's door flung open. Even the face of a tiger would not have looked fiercer than his.

The rope slipped off Gangi's clutch. The pitcher along with the rope fell with a thud down into the water of the well. And for several moments, sounds of massive bellowing were being heard from the water.

The Thakur was rushing towards the well roaring with *'kaun hai, kaun hai'*. And Gangi had jumped off the raised curb of the well and was running away for life. As she reached her home, she saw Jokhu was drinking that fetid water only, putting his mouth into the *lota.*

❒

3. THE DEPENDENT BRIDEGROOM
(Ghar Jawai)

Haridhan Seth returned in the noon after having the sugarcane field watered and sat outside the house. Smoke was seen coming out from inside the household. Also were heard the jingling sounds from it. Both his two brothers-in-law came behind him and entered the household. Sons of both the brothers-in-law came too and went inside; but Haridhan could not go inside. For the last one month the treatment he was meted out here, and yesterday in particular the scoldings that he had, were like fetters round his feet. Only yesterday his mother-in-law had said: 'I am fed up with you. Well have I to shoulder all your burden for your life?' Most of all this besides, the cruelty he faced from his wife had broken his heart into pieces. She sat there listening to all scoldings but never once came from her mouth the words of objection like: 'Why Amma you do insult him like that'. She only kept on seated all the while. 'Perhaps she was deriving pleasures from my discomfiture.' How then could he enter such a household? Well, for the similar abuses or for some further reprimands? 'And such miserable is my state that even after having spent ten years of my life with this family? Do I work less than anybody here? Both the brothers-in-law enjoy comfortable siesta while I remain yoked in feeding the bulls, in prunings. Every day when they smoke from their chhelum time and again—resting, I remain busy in my works keeping my eyes away from them. Every day in the evening the folks and their families go out for entertainment, while I continue milking the cows and buffaloes until late in the night. The reward for all this I'm given is that nobody even asks me for food. On the contrary, abuses are hurled at me.'

His wife came out with a pail and ordered: "Fetch some water from the well. Not a drop of water is there in the house."

Haridhan picked up the pail and fetched water from the well. He was very hungry. He thought any moment he would be called in for his meal, but his wife simply took up the pail of water and remained there inside, unconcerned of him. Haridhan, exhausted from hard labour, afflicted with hunger, lay there as if asleep.

All of a sudden his wife Gumani came out and woke him up. Haridhan asked from his laid posture: "What is it? Won't you even allow me sleep or you want me fetch some more water?"

In rude overtone Gumani replied: "Why grumble? I have come to call you in for food."

Right at that moment Haridhan noticed both his brothers-in-law and the two sons of the eldest going out after having their meals. He became sad. 'I'm not allowed to dine even along with these people? They are my masters! I'm only to live on licking their left-overs! I'm like their dogs, which are given crumbs after they have left them over? And this is the household where ten years back he was treated with great hospitality. All in the family behaved as though they were his slaves. The mother-in-law used to look for him. His wife would worship him. At that time he had money, lands too. But now he was poor. These people turned all his property into garbage. Now he was too tight even to two square meals a day. A seething anger surged up in his heart so much that he felt like burning inside that very moment to thrash his mother-in-law and wife, right and left, but he only exercised restraints instead. From his laid down posture only he replied to Gumani: "I'm not hungry. I won't take food today."

Gumani said: "Damn I care whether you eat or not; yes, I mean it. Something will go into your stomach if you eat, and not mine anyway?"

The seething anger in Haridhan turned into tears. 'This is my wife for whom I have spent off all my resources I had. Having already befooled me these fellows now want to oust me altogether. But where would I go now? What'd I do?'

His mother-in-law came out to ask: "Why don't you come in for your meal? To whom are you showing off all your tempers? We don't have the appetite to stand your coquetry. The bits whatever you give, well, don't give that any longer, what else can you do hence? We have married our daughter to you alright but that of course does not mean we've taken any vow to look after you all your life?"

Stunned Haridhan said: "Yes mother, my mistake was that I began to think like that. What after all I'm left with now that you'd feel tempted to look after me for life? When I had wealth everything was forthcoming. Now that I'm resourceless, why after all you'd think for me?"

His old mother-in-law also returned with a face wry at his answer.

2

To the children their father is generally a nonentity—a thing of luxury—as gram is to horses or *mohan bhog* to babus. If one's deprived of *roti-dal, mohan bhog* all his life, who's there to suffer any loss? But if one day one doesn't get his *roti-dal,* see what happens? The father is available both the times, in the mornings and in the evenings. He tosses his children upwards, while fondling caresses them, sometimes takes them out for rounds holding them close to his bosom, or by holding them by fingers and that's all, there ends his duties. If he goes away even to far-off places they do not bother. But the mother is everything for children. A boy cannot stand separation from her even for a moment. Whoever be his father he doesn't mind very much, he must only be able to toss him upwards while fondling or be able to make him romp and jump in merriment. But the mother is his own, absolutely own, same colours, same fondling, same everything. If she is not present the undercurrent of the child's liveliness gets withered. Then he turns to become like Nandi, the associate vagabond with the Lord Shiva, rearing whom with nutriments or care becomes not merely essential, but righteous.

It was ten years since Haridhan's mother had died. He was married at that time. He was sixteen only. But soon his mother's death he realised: 'How hapless am I'. He as it were had lost all his claim in the household whatsoever. His sisters were married off too by then. He had no brother. The poor thing was afraid even of entering the household. He used to lament for his mother yet was scared of her mother's shadow. The room where she had breathed her last, he would not even look into. There he had an aunt too, who used to dote upon him. As for his share of the milk, Haridhan was getting that more now, and the duties he was given to do were much less. The aunt would ask him time and again: 'My child, would you like to have some more food?' Even his father had began caring more for him then onwards. He bought a separate cow for him. At times he would give him even money, so he might spend as he wished. But the balms as were these would not heal the wounds he had, and that had been afflicting his soul. The dotage and the cares would only remind him of his dear mother time and again instead. There was not as much pleasure in such dotage as were in his mother's feigning rebuffs. The pleasures he used to derive at getting anything from his mother after quarrels, or whining or by sulking, could they be in such charities? Earlier as he used to eat by asking and after quarrels he kept on good health; but now despite having been given better foods, he was sickly, he did not have enough appetite.

For a whole year he remained in such state of mind. Then the world changed for him. A new woman, whom people called his mother, came in the family, and by and by something ominous overcast his little world—shadow of darkness veiled over all his verdure, all the lights he was seeing. Never did Haridhan speak to that new mother, never did he even go close to her. One day he moved out of his home and came to his in-laws.

His father called for him repeatedly; yet as long as he was alive he did not go home. The day when he heard of his father's death, he felt a sort of jealous delight. Even a drop of tears did not appear in his eyes.

Having arrived at this new household Haridhan once again relished mother's affection. Like a boon from a sage his mother-in-law filled his life with magnificence. The desert got vegetated. Amid cajoling his sister-in-law, affection from the mother-in-law, with grandiloquence of his brothers-in-law and from love of his wife, he found all his life's desires fulfilled. The mother-in-law had said: "Son, consider this household as yours. You are only the apple of my eyes." She would complaint with him of her sons and daughters-in-law. From his heart he began to think that *'Sasji* likes me even more than her sons'.

Soon as his father had died, he had gone home, squandered his shares in the property to return with bagful of rupees. As a result whatever hospitality he was since been given to taste had got doubled. Having bestowed all his resources upon the feet of his mother-in-law he felt his life was gratified. Before long he used to think of his home nostalgically every now and then, but gradually it stopped occurring in his mind, even by mistake, as if that was a terrible episode in his life, and thereby forgetting which after all was the better for him. He would rise earliest of all, work more than anybody. Having observed his concentration and industry, the villagers would bite their fingers in astonishment. They would all be of praise of the luck his father-in-law had in getting a son-in-law as was he.

But as days passed on, the warm hospitality he was being given began waning. First he was a god, then a member in the family, and lastly, a servant in the household. Even food was not easily forthcoming. He began feeling insulted. If the folks in the family were starving, and consequently if he too were required to starve along with them, he won't ever have grudged wee bit about it. But as he found them safe and secure, and it was only he reduced to be an unwanted entity, a long cold sigh of grief emanated from the core of his heart. He was only twenty four now. How would he lead the rest long period of his life? At this household? Crowning all her miseries was his wife who also had turned her face away from him. That was the cruellest side of his misfortune.

3

Outside Haridhan was being famished with hunger and thirst, while inside the house the *sasji* and his brothers-in-law were busy in talks. Gumani also was chiming in with them.

The eldest brother-in-law said: "He wants to equal us, but he fails to realise that nobody here has taken up his responsibility for life. Ten years have gone by, well, he must have already usurped two-three thousand rupees during the period, no?"

The youngest brother-in-law joined in: "If he were a labourer then one could even snub him or scold, but him?—who has the cheek to tell him anything? None knows if we would be able to get rid of the oblation to a man as he. Perhaps he thinks 'have I not given them my two thousand rupees'—but he does not care to understand that his two thousand bucks have long been vanquished. Well, even for one time meal he consumes one and a-half seer of foodstuff."

The *sasji* agreed to add with gravity: "That's burdensome for one's diet.

Gumani was pinching out lice from her mother's hairs. Burning inwardly she said: "There's no work for an indolent man have eating."

The eldest joined: 'Well, as for meals there is no grudge. One would eat as much as he would feel hungry, but he should earn something too. This fellow does not realise that his days are spent here as our guest only."

The younger: "One day I would tell him blatantly,— now you should mind your own way, we have not been indebted to you!

As she heard her kins in the family talk in such manners, Gumani used her mind to behave rancorous to her husband. Had he been bringing home something earned from outside, she would have had greater esteem in her family. She too could have lived queenly. Who knows why he feels like getting lost in going out to earn a livelihood. Gumani's mentality was childish still, thoroughly. She did not have a home as her own. For her now her mother's home was the main resort, be it good or evil. Alike them she too spoke the same language for a thought, used to see a problem in identical light as her kins in the family would do. the truth is could you buy every body by two thousand rupees? After all what was the value of two thousand rupees in ten years? It's only two hundred a year! Well, for the whole year the two persons won't even eat food worth two hundred rupees? Besides, there are also expenses for clothings, milk, ghee, etc.? Ten years have passed since their marriage, even a brass ringlet was not made for her. He would feel like losing heart when it came to going out for livelihood. He thinks that he would continue to get adoration here all his life like he used to get before. He won't appreciate that things were different before and something other now. Besides, it's the bride who goes to her in-law's in the first place, and is given excellent reception. Soon as she steps down from the palanquin, musical instruments are played, women from the village and the locality throng around to have a look at her face and pay money as gifts. For months she is given good food at the household, good clothings to wear, no work is taken from her. But after six months, nobody cares for her, she is rendered to become a maid in the family. In his home I would have met with such eventuality anyway. Then why do you lament that you would claim 'I work for the household? Well then it's your mistake. Talk of a labourer however is a different issues. Owner scolds him, thrashes him, keeps him in the employment as and when pleases. Work is taken of him coercively. Not like yours that you'd work as you'd please, or lay down sleeping whenever you would wish.

4

Haridhan was now fuming to himself as both his brothers-in-law came out and the eldest said: 'Brother, get up. The afternoon is almost spent off, how long would you go on sleeping? The entire field is lying as barren.'

Instantly Haridhan got up and pat came his reply in fierce overtone: "What! You all have taken me for an idiot?"

Both the brothers-in-law were taken aback. A fellow who never uttered a word, who always presented himself at beck and call like a slave, the same one could acquire so much self-esteem, all so suddenly, was enough to startle them. Any reply was not found out.

As Haridhan noticed, these two were rendered staggering, he could not hold a strong temptation to give them another jolt. He continued in the same vein: "Well, I'm not blind, I've my eyes too, nor am I a deaf. Would I be required to put in rigorous labour, and then even after that would be treated like a dog? Well, well, I'm not such an ass."

The eldest brother-in-law fumed up: "Nobody however has confined you here."

This made Haridhan speechless. He could not find an answer.

The eldest spoke again in the same overtone: “If you want to stay as a guest all your life and continue to think that you’ll be given similar hospitality, well then that is beyond our capability.”

Goggling his eyes in anger Haridhan said: “What! You want to say I work less than what you all do!”

The eldest: “Who says that?”

Haridhan: “So the practice in your family is one who works the most should die in hunger?”

The eldest: “You yourself did not go inside to eat. Well, should someone put morsels into your mouth?”

Haridhan said biting his lip: “I didn’t go to eat? Don’t you feel ashamed telling this?”

—“Didn’t our sister come to take you in?”

Blood came in Haridhan’s eye out of fury, gnashing his teeth he was left to fume.

The younger brother-in-law joined in: “Even mother had come to call you inside. You had refused saying ‘I don’t have appetite for food’. What then she should have done?”

The mother-in-law was coming out from indoors with strides. Having overheard their talks she said sharply: “I got disappointed after calling him for so many times. If he won’t get up what would I do in that condition?”

His voice messed up in poisonous-bloody and furious feelings as Haridhan replied: “Why? Am I to live on left-overs of your sons? Am I a dog that after having finished your own meals you would drop the crumbs before me to live on?”

Conceitedly the old woman asked: “What! Would you like to equal my sons?”

Haridhan was defeated. With slapping of one word she had destroyed him. The outstretched world he thought he had slackened. The fire in his eyes vanquished, the throbbing nostrils calmed. Like a wounded man he fell down on earth. The sentence—‘What! Would you like to equal my sons?’—was as if a lance piercing his heart, nothing was left of the heart nor of the lance.

5

All the members of the family ate their meals, but Haridhan did not get up. The *sas* came to persuade, the sister-in-law tried to appease, the father-in-law mollified and both the brother-in-law tried to pacify him, then resigned. Haridhan did not rise. A floormat was there abandoned. He picked that up, carried near the well, spread it on the raised circular curb of the well and lay there down.

The night had turned colder. The bright stars in the firmament began playing like young boys. Some of them were dancing, some jumping, some were laughing and some blinking only to open up the next moment. By fits and starts some of the boys were covering that vast expanse in a moment of expeditious move and vanishing no one knows where. Haridhan recollected his childhood when he too used to play like this. The memoirs were enkindled in him as were the bright stars. That small house of his, those mango groves where he used to go to collect unripe mangoes, that field where he used to play kabaddi crowded in his memory lane. Then came up in his vision a care-torn image of his mother. How great was the compassion in those eyes. How immense was the kindness. He seemed to envision as if his mother was approaching with tears in her eyes, her hands spread forward to cling him to her bosom. With that honeyed feelings suddenly he lost himself. He felt, as though, his mother had embraced him closely, and was stroking his head with loving concerns. He began weeping, effusively. In the self-deluded state following words came out from his mouth: 'Mother how much have you forgotten me. Come and see what is the plight of your dear son. Nobody asks him even a glass of water. Can't you find room for me at yours where you live now.'

Suddenly Gumani came out calling: "Well, have you slept already? Oh, God should forbid that anybody should have capacity of such demonic sleep as you go to! Why can't you come in and have your meal? How long should one keep sitting in wait for you?"

From his fancied other world, Haridhan dropped on to the cruel reality. It was the same circular raised curb around the well, the same tattered floor-mat, and Gumani, standing in front of him snubbing: "How long should one be sitting in wait for you?"

Haridhan got up promptly and like drawing out a sword from its sheath spoke: "Good, at last you got reminded of me. Have I not said that I do not have appetite for food?"

Gumani: "Well, then how many days will you avoid food?"

—"From now onwards I won't even drink a glass of water at this household. Tell me now, would you like to come out along with me or not?"

His determined words made Gumani nervous. She asked: "Where are you going?"

Haridhan replied: "That's none of your business. Will you accompany me or you won't? Don't complain afterwards that I did not ask you."

With an overtone to object, Gumani asked: "Why don't you tell me where are you going exactly?"

—"Oh, would you come along with me or not?"

—"As long as you won't tell me, I won't tell you so."

—"So it is now well known that you would not like to come along with me. I waited here to ask you only this much, or by this time I would have covered almost half way through."

Having said this he stood up and moved out towards his old home. Gumani continued calling from behind: "Oh, listen, please,"—but never once he looked back.

6

The stretch of thirty miles of his destination Haridhan covered in five hours. As he reached near the mango- groves near his village, his feelings of his mother-land were happily ensconsed in the golden lap of dawn. At the sight of those trees his agitated heart began to dance. As he spotted the golden pitcher atop the temple, he ran towards that direction in such rashness as if, he would take a long leap to land upon it. He was running with a rash that seemed as if his mother was there drawing him to her care-torn embrace. As he entered the mango-groves, in branches of which he once used himself to seat fancying joyful elephant ride, where in the green unripe mangoes and their *lasarh* he used to get heavenly relish, he sat there down and placing his head down upon the earth he began to cry, as it were, he was telling his mother of his tales of miseries. In the air at that place, in that light, as if, the vastness of his mother was spreading up all around. Every finger-tip of that land seemed more pious than even the foot-steps of his mother. Although the firmament there he heard the echoes of his care-torn mother's words. No one knows what was the rejuvenating factor there, in that air, in that part of the firmament, which once again filled his aggrieved soul with puerile exuberance. He climbed up in one of that trees and plucked the mangoes. He began eating them yearningly. The harsh words from his mother-in-law, his wife's cruel blows, all the insults he had forgotten. His feet had swollen, in soles was burning sensation, but amid his delight he cared for none of these.

All of a sudden the keeper of the groves shouted at him: 'Who's climbing up there? Get down right away or I'll fling stones at you so you would remain there afixed, dead cold.'

He also hurled a few abuses at him. Yet from his rebukes and abuses Haridhan got transcendental pleasures. Behind the branches he hid himself plucked a few mangoes, downed them there and burst into laughter. He realised that moment that long he did not laugh such bursting laughter as well.

To the keeper his laughter sounded familiar. But how Haridhan could be there, he surmised. Well, he was at his in-laws', eating bread of idleness. He was the only fellow who would dive down into the pool from atop a tree. Who else could be in the village now behaving like him?

He said: 'If you go on laughing like this from there I would rush onto you and break all your teeth. Get down at once and come here.'

His railings were on when promptly a stone came in straight and hit his head. "Who's there the wicked, not budging? Okay, you wait there; here I come to hit you now."

He left his stick beneath the tree and climbed up onto it with a monkey's skill, and there he found Haridhan, grinning at him. Surprised he asked: "How come; well, well, it's Haridhan. When did you come here? Since when you ensconsed yourself into this tree?"

They were two childhood companions. They embraced each other there itself.

—"Well, have you returned now only? Come along, come to your home. Oh, you the goodman, even mangoes you were not been able to get there?"

Smiling, Haridhan replied: "Mangru, the taste these mangoes have, you won't find in mangoes at any other place. Now, tell me what are the ways of the village?"

Mangru: "All are quiet and at peace there. As for you, you seemed to have snapped all relationship. Should anybody have to leave one's home and village like you did? Ever since your father died entire household got disturbed. There are two young boys. What could they be able to have done?"

Haridhan: "Now brother, I do not have any connection with that family. I have already settled all my claims with them. Well, I will get a job of labourer here, no? At least I can be employed to take your cattle for grazing, just you give me the fooding in return of that."

Unbelieving Mangru replied: "Oh, what shocking things are you telling? I can lay my life down for you. Well, would you not live at your in-laws any longer? Never worry then. In the first place, you have your own household. Take charge of that. Little are the children there, groom them up. For nothing were you scared of your new mother. She is quite simple. Only you should consider her as your mother. She will be delighted having got you back there. Well then, will you also bring your wife back, right?"

Haridhan: "I won't even look at her face now onwards. For me she is dead."

Mangru: "Very well, you will marry then for the second time. Now we will get you such a bride that you'll feel gratified enough to feel even do worship her, but what if your first wife comes back too?"

Haridhan: "She will never come."

7

As Haridhan arrived his home, his two younger brothers chanted aloud, 'Bhaiya has come, Bhaiya has come', dashed inside to inform their mother.

Soon as he entered that room glorious peace instilled in him as if he was placed ensconced in his mother's lap. His heart had softened after being kicked about for such long time of his life. Earlier he had vanity, pertinacity, stubbornness, in place of all these he now had hopelessness and defeat. The mental ill-health was fast losing its grip on him now, even a trifle measure of cure could act on him. The walls of his fortress had now holes, it was not impossible to enter in him. The same household that he had left once for all having been fed up with it, was today ready with open arms to give him shelter, Haridhan's shelterless heart as it were got satisfied at this refuge.

At the dusk his step-mother said: "Son, you have returned home, we are very fortunate. Now groom up these little boys.

They are kins to you from your father's side of course, if only you do not accept them from your mother's side as well. Just throw little bits of food to me daily, I'll live happily in one corner, unconcerned. My relation with your dead mother is one of a sister. From that point of relationship, you are my son too."

In her perplexed care-torn eyes, Haridhan saw the image of his own mother in the form of the step-mother. In every corner of the house reminiscences of her mother were reflected like moonlight, and the middle-aged countenance of his stepmother was aglow in that light.

The next day once again Haridhan rested the plough on his shoulders and moved towards the field. Elation was reflected from his face and pride spilled forth from his eyes. No longer he was a dependent on anybody, he was a patron now. Nor was he a beggar at one's doorstep, he was a protector of his house.

One day he heard, Gumani had set up a home with some other fellow. To his mother he spoke of that: "Have you heard Kaki? Gumani has set up a home with someone else."

His Kaki replied: "It's only a joke. How can she set up a house with someone else? Such an outrage in the family? If there is no panchayat, at least there is court of law for justice."

Haridhan answered: "Well, well, no Kaki. Whatever has happened is for good. Give me money, I will buy *laddoos* to offer to Mahabirji in gratitude. In fact, I was afraid that she might come back to become a burden for me. God has heard my prayers. I have left them for good with a resolve that hence onwards I would not even look at her face."

❒

4. A NIGHT OF POOSE
(Poose ki Raat)

Halku came to his wife to say: 'Sahna is at the door. The money you have kept aside, give that. I want to pay him off to get rid of him.'

Munni was busy at sweeping. Turning back she replied: 'We have only three rupees left, if you pay that off to him, how the blanket would be bought? How would we be able to spend the nights of *magh* and *poose* at the *haar*? Tell him rather, we'd pay him after the harvest. Not now.'

For a moment Halku stood there undecided. *Poose*, the last of the two months of winter, is almost arrived. Without a blanket they would not be able to sleep at the *haar* by any means. But Sahna won't agree, he would rebuff instead, hurl abuses. Oh damn it, we'd better die in cold, at least we'd be able to get rid of that evil. Thinking so with his heavy serious stature, which proved his name false, he came closer to his wife and in faltering overtone said: 'Come, give me that. Let's get rid of him. As for the blanket we'd find out some other way.'

Munni drifted herself away from him and replied with admonishing glance: 'Well, enough of that other ways. Very well, tell me for a moment, which other way have you been able to find out? Will anybody give you that as a dole? None knows how much is the balance that we will have to pay off—the balance which never comes to an end, any how. I ask you instead, why don't you leave farming? You work and die on it, yet after the harvest everything is spent in paying off the balance—leave it, get rid of such kind of farming. No, I won't give the money, I won't.'

Halku asked gloomily: 'So, have I to withstand his abuses?'

Aggressively Munni countered: 'Why would he hurl abuses? Is it his rule here?'

But simultaneous to her telling so, her twisted eyebrows slackened.

The harsh truth that was there in Halku's utterance, was haunting her like a terrible animal.

She went to the racks, fetched the money and put that onto the palm of Halku. Then said: 'From now onward you better forsake doing farming. From a manual labour's wages we can at least peacefully have pittance for a living. At least we won't have to bear anyone's coercive blusterings. And what a good farming it is! Work your heart out to earn, and thereafter consign whatever you have earned into them and also tolerate blusterings on top of that.'

Halku accepted the money and went outside with such demeanour as if he was going to pluck his heart out for payment. Saving farthings from his wages, one by one, he had accumulated three rupees for a blanket. That amount was to be removed. With every step his head seemed being downpressed under the weight of his destitution.

2

It was a dark night of *poose.* Even stars in the firmament looked shuddering with cold. Wrapped in his old coarse wrapper, Halku was lying shivering on a bamboo-cot placed at a corner of his field, under the roof of sugarcane leaves. Under the cot his all-time companion, a dog, Jabrah, was groaning in cold with his mouth pressed into his own belly for warmth. None of the two was getting sleep.

Having coiled himself up by pressing his throat to his knees, Halku said: 'Jabrah, do you feel the cold now? I was asking you to lay there at home on the straw bed, but you didn't. What had you been thinking to get here? Alright taste the cold now, what can you do otherwise? Perhaps you thought I'm coming here to eat *halwa-puri,* so you came running ahead of me. Alright, now you cry calling out for your dear grandma.'

Lying there as he was Jabrah wagged his tail, prolonged its groan, yawned and then lay silent. Perhaps he got snub from its canine intelligence that the master was not getting sleep because of his groaning.

Halku brought out one hand to rub its back gently saying: 'Don't come along with me from tomorrow or you might get frozen. Ah! this witchy westerly wind, God knows from where does it bring the icy chill. Let me get up, make one more *chelum.* Let the night be spent somehow. Eight *chelums* I've already smoked off. Ah! this is the fun of tilling. And, there lies another god, the owner of the field, whom even if the winter goes to engulf it would be repelled by his warmth. The thick mattresses, quilt, blanket; can winter dare to enter there? What a luck! The labour I would do, but the fruit of that somebody else would enjoy!'

Halku got up, poked out some fire from a pit, and made the *chelum.* Jabrah got up and sat too.

While dragging from his *chelum,* Halku asked him: 'Why? Like to have a drag from the *chelum?* Well, the cold would not vanquish, but of course, you might have a change of mind for a while.'

Jabrah stared at his master's face with liquid eyes.

Halku: 'Alright, stand this cold today somehow. From tomorrow I would get you some straw here spread for you. You may thrust yourself, be ensconced in that and there won't be any more cold then.'

Jabrah put the paws upon his knees and brought his mouth close to his master's. Halku felt his warm breath.

Having had his fill into the *chelum,* Halku lay down again, and with the resolve 'now must I sleep anyhow'. But the very next moment his heart began shuddering with cold. Now he would turn this side, then the other, yet the winter like an evil spirit was there hard pressed onto his chest.

But when he failed to stand that any longer, silently he woke up Jabrah, with patterings on its head, he dragged him onto his lap made him lay there to sleep. From his body came the unknown stinks, yet holding the dog firmly into his lap he sensed such pleasures that for months those days he was not getting. Perhaps Jabrah was thinking it was the heaven, and in the pious heart of Halku there was not a streak of hatred toward the dirty dog. Even a bosom friend of his or a brother he would have embraced with such readiness. He was not offended at his poverty, which had rendered him to such plight. No, this unique friendship, as if, had opened all the doors of his soul and each and every particle of his was dazzling with light.

Suddenly, Jabrah heard of footsteps of some animal. The new relationship had already injected in him new energy so much that it helped him treat the cold blasts of the wind with neglect. He sprang up, pat came he out of the thatched roof, barking. Several times Halku called him in with caressing sounds, but he did not return to him. All round the tilling area he ran barking. If ever he would come for a while, the next moment again he would go back running. Sense of duty was surging in his heart like fond hopes.

3

Another hour was spent thus. Night further intensified the cold infusing in it the wind. Halku got up to sit, folded up his knees, joined them together to press hard against his chest and thrust his head between, to hide from cold wind, yet the cold did not minimise. It appeared that all his blood had frozen.

In his arteries snow was flowing instead of blood. He craned his neck upwards to see the sky, to find out how much of night was still left. The Great Bear had not yet ascended half its assigned place. It would be dawn only after it ascended right atop. It was still night for even more than a *pahar*.

Close to the field of Halku, in the vicinity, was a mangrove. The season of defoliation was on. Dry leaves were there in heaps in the grove. Halku decided: 'Let me pick up some dry mango-leaves and make a fire to warm up to my comfort. But if somebody spots me assorting the dry leaves, he may take me to be an apparition. Who knows there even be some animal hidden there; yet it's intolerable to sit like this any longer.'

He walked to the nearby pigeon pea field, uprooted some of the plants and made a broom out of them, then holding in his hand an ignited cow-dung cake he moved toward the grove. Jabrah found him return, came closer and began wagging his tail.

Halku said: 'Now it's intolerable, Jabru! Come, we will pile up the dry leaves in the grove and warm ourselves from its fire. After we have warmed up we would come here back to sleep. It's still quite night.'

Jabrah groaned in agreement and moved ahead toward the grove. The grove was completely darkened, and in that darkness ruthless wind was smashing through the leaves. The dew drops were falling down from trees in quick drips.

Suddenly a blast of wind wafted in fragrance from myrtle flowers. Halku said: 'What a fragrance my dear Jabru! Are you smelling some aroma?'

Jabrah had got a bone lying somewhere. He was busy in sucking it holding between his teeth.

Halku put the fire down on earth and then set down to assort the dried leaves; in a few moments piles of leaves were assorted. His hands were shivering in cold. His bare feet were being frost-bitten while he continued to amass heaps of leaves. As if, in that bonfire he would burn off the cold.

The bonfire caught flames in a few moments. Its flames were rising up to touch now the leaves high atop the trees and in the next moment would vanish. In that unsteady light the big tree of the garden looked like balancing on its head entire masses of darkness. And amidst that boisterous sea of darkness, this tiny light appeared tossed around and crumbled.

In front of the bonfire Halku was warming himself up. One moment he wriggled off his garment and held it in his armpit, stretched his legs out to enjoy the warmth, as it were, he was challenging the winter, 'do whatever you would please'. Having won over the enormous might of the winter, he was not being able to hold his triumph.

To Jabrah he said: 'Why Jabbar! Now you don't feel cold, no?'

With his groan Jabrah seemed replying: 'Should one feel cold even now?'

—'I din't think of this before, or we won't have tasted so much of cold so long.'

Jabrah wagged his tail in response.

—'Okay come, let us compete in jumping over this bonfire. Let us see who pips whom. Mind you my child, if you scorch yourself I won't give you medical treatment.'

Jabrah looked at that flaming fire in solicitous eyes. 'Don't tell Munni of this tomorrow, she would fight with me.'

Speaking thus he jumped and made clean over the bonfire. Flames slightly scorched his feet, but that was nothing. Jabrah took a round of the fire instead and came beside him.

Halku said: 'Oh come on, this is not the right process. You have to come jumping over it.' He jumped thereafter, and came this side crossing over the fire.

The leaves were burnt out. The grove was once again under darkness. A little fire was still under the ashes, which was stoked up by occasional whiff of wind. Next moment afterward it would close its eyes once again.

Halku wore the wrapper round him once again seated beside that warm ashes he began humming; but as cold grew on, he got subdued by exhaustion.

Jabrah suddenly howled at something and rushed toward the field. Halku felt like a herd of animals was in the field. Probably there was the herd of *neelgai.* Sounds from their romp and jumps were coming clear to his ears, then suddenly he made it that they were grazing in the field. He even heard sounds of their munching— *charrh, charrh.*

From his heart he spoke: 'No as long as Jabrah is there the animals cannot dare to graze in the field. He will scratch them. I must be having some illusion at present. Well where! Nothing can I hear now. Oh, what a deception I had!'

Loud he shouted: "Jabrah, Jabrah.'

Jabrah continued his barking. Didn't come back to him.

Again sounds of grazing in the field came loud to his ears. Now he could not falsely assure himself any longer. It was as though the feel of poison for him to move from his ensconce. How firmly he had seated himself. Going to the field in mid-winter, running after animals thrashing them were intolerable job for him. He did not move from his place.

Louder he shouted: Hilo! Hilo! Hilo!'

Once again Jabrah barked aloud. Animals were grazing in the field. The crops were ripe. What a good crop was it; but the devilish animals were deavouring them, destroying them all.

Halku got up now with sound resolve and walked forward a few steps; but right at that moment a sudden chilly, prickly blast of wind blew, such poisonous stinging was it that forthwith he returned to that dying fire and poked the living ashes to try to warm his body.

Jabrah was barking at the top of his voice, while the *neelgais* were eating away the crops of the field clean and Halku was ensconced peacefully in the warmth of the dying fire.

He was as if tied all around his body to captivity by threads of disinclination to react.

On the warm spot near that dying ashes he spread his wrapper and fell asleep.

As he woke up in the morning, all round there was bright sun and Munni was calling him: 'Why, would you lay asleep like this? You came here for comfort while there in the field entire crop was rendered to ruin.'

Standing up Halku said: 'What! Are you coming from the field?'

Munni replied: 'Yes, entire field has been rendered to devastation. Well, should anybody sleep like as you did? What is the result from your night watch, from that thatched pavilion?'

Halku argued: 'Oh, I got my life back from almost certain death. And you are crying over the field? Such was the ache in my stomach, such severe pains, that I alone know.'

Thereafter both rushed to the ridge of the field. They saw entire field was trampled to ruin and Jabrah was lying under the thatched pavilion on his back, turned turtle, as if there was not even life in him.

Both were witnessing plight of the field. Dejection was writ large on Munni's face, but Halku looked happy.

Anxious, Munni suggested: 'Now onwards we will have to work as daily wager labourers for our living.'

With happy countenance Halku answered: 'Well, at least we won't have to sleep in the chill of the winter nights.'

❐

5. A TABLEAU
(Jhanki)

For a few days last bickerings were rife in the household. Mother was seated aside with a wry face, and the wife ensconced at another side. The atmosphere of the household was as if poisoned. Dinner was not cooked; in the day I had prepared *khichdi* on the stove, but nobody ate that. Even the children did not have the appetite today. The youngest daughter would often come to me and then to her mother or the grandmother; but nowhere were loving words for her today. Nobody would lift her onto lap, as it were, she had done a crime. The son returned from the school in the afternoon. Nobody gave him food to eat, neither spoke to him nor asked him if he wanted anything. Both the children got seated in the verandah in pensive mood and perhaps were wondering why all at home have turned their hearts away from them. How many times in a day they—the brother and the sister—had fought with each other, many times there took place weeping and wailing—but never so happened in the home that meals were not cooked or one did not speak to others. What kind of a quarrel was it? That even after passing twenty- four hours of the day, it did not subside? This perhaps would not figure in their mind.

There was no basis of the quarrel indeed. My mother wanted some items to enlist in the gifts to be presented to my sister for *teej,* which considering the pecuniary conditions of the household seemed excessive to my wife.

My *amma* herself was considerate enough. She on her own had curtailed some of the items. But according to my wife's views some further curtailment should have been done. In place of five sarees three were enough; what was wrong in it? Why so many toys? What was the utility in sending so much of sweetmeats? Her opinion was—since enough did not come from earnings, one should tighten the day to day expenses; if the budget for the daily milk and butter was now squeezed then why so much liberalisation with the *teej?* One should light up one's own home first, the mosque outside thereafter. But here in this household this did not happen—the mosque was to be lighted up anyhow, the home might ever lurch in darkness. Differences grew between the *Sas* and the *bahu* on this point. Gradually individual faults were found out. The quarrels spread from the genesis to elsewhere and old subdued disputes were dug out afresh. Then came turns for allegorical jeers at one another, taunts were hurled in series aplenty and everything ended up in figures of speechlessness.

I was in predicament. If I sided with mother and said something in her favour, my dear wife would start her weeps and laments cursing her fate; and if I spoke for my wife then I got the ill-fame of becoming a stickler to the wife. I, therefore, was supporting both by turns; but for my own selfish reasons my sympathy went with my wife only. As for my cinema budget it was totally vanished of late; even the expenses of betel et cetera. I was required to minimise; outings in the market place hence got stopped. I was not been able to confide my problems in my mother frankly; but I used to be under impression by my heart that the austerity measures were her deeds only.

The state of my shop was such that at times I would not get even the first sale of the day. Money were not realised from the clients, hence why one should put oneself into distress by following all these traditional rituals?

Time and again my heart used to get irritated at this shambles of my household. A few heads only live in the family but even then there was no fellow-feeling among them. Such household one should hurl into fires. At times I used to be guided by some caprice that I should abandon everything and flee away somewhere else. These people would come to their senses only when responsibility would fall all upon their heads. They would learn only thereafter how household should be run. Who knew that I would be required to tackle such troubles, or I would never have even thought of marrying at all. Several untoward thoughts were recurring in my mind. It's only *amma* who wanted to trouble me, and nothing else—I conjectured. If her *bahu* weren't to massage her feet, won't rub her head with hairoil, how these could come to be my faults? I never asked her not to do that? I would, in fact, have got real pleasures if *sas-bahu* developed such concerns toward each other; but I never had the capability to instill sense of fellow-feeling into them. If *amma* in her youth had to wash sarees of her mother-in-law, or massage her feet, had to swallow brow-beatings, then why such old scores she must have to settle with her own *bahu*? Why can't she see that time has changed. Today's daughters- in-law do not drudge upon their mothers-in-law out of any fear. With love you might even manage to pluck hairs from their heads today, but days for trying to rein over them by overawing are gone.

Entire township that day was celebrating Janmashtami. At my home there was battle royal on. It was already evening, yet at my household it was all dark. Gloom had cast its spell. I got angry with my wife. If you so desire to fight, okay do that; why have you put the household lurching in darkness? I went close to her to ask: Well, won't there be any light tonight?

My wife retorted sulking: Why don't you light yourself? Don't you have your hands?

Angered sparked in me. I countered: What! When you had not come into our family, were there no lamps used to be lighted those days?

Amma played stoking the fire, saying: Oh no never! Those days we used to grope in the darkness only.

Infuriated by such a taunt from mother, my dear wife got out of her bounds. She thundered: Maybe you were burning oil from the lamps of clay? I haven't seen a lantern in this household. And ten years has been spent since.

I snubbed her: Alright now keep quiet. Don't go beyond a limit.

—Ha! You snub me as if you have brought me by bargain.

—Silence, I say!

—Why should I be silent! If you tell me one, be ready to get two in return.

—Is it the style of your loyalty?

—As be the peeve, so'd be the challenge.

Vanquished I came outside, and then seated in a dark room I began cursing that ominous hour when I got married to this woman of disposition. Even in that darkness ten years of my married life ran through flashing upon the canvas of my memory like a cinematic picture. There was no flash of light anywhere in it, no softness of love.

2

All of a sudden Pandit Jaydevji, who is my friend as well, came to the door and spoke out on top of his voice: Hey folks, why such darkness here? Nothing is visible. Where you are all?

I did not reply, wondering from where this man emerged to fall upon my shoulders.

Jaydev shouted again calling: Well, where are you brother? Why don't you reply? Is there anyone in the house or not?

He did not get any answer from anybody.

Jaydev jerked the door with so much force that I got afraid the door might crumble down with all its door-frame and sides pulled out. Yet I did not speak. His arrival was pricking me like thorns.

Jaydev went away. I breathed relief. An attacking devil seemed dissuaded, or for hours he would have plagued me with his blabs.

But within five minutes, once again I heard somebody's footsteps and this time a powerful focus from a torch flooded my entire interior. Having spotted me seated Jaydev asked curiously—Where had you been dear? For hours I have shouted calling you, none even cared to reply? What is all this affairs here today? Why the lamps are not lighted?

I feigned: I don't know why. I had headache, came home from the shop to lie down and fell asleep.

—And you went to go into a deep carefree sleep, as if never again to wake up.

—Yes, my friend, I had fallen asleep.

—Yet lamps should have been lighted in the house, or have you even declared 'retrenchment' for them?

—Today in the house, people are on fast. May be they're all too busy.

—Alright leave these. Are you coming to see the *jhanki?* There at Seth Ghureylal's a *jhanki* has been constructed such beautiful that one cannot turn his eyes away from it. Such glassmade and electrical equipments have been decorated in it that eyes glisten at it. There is a fare of red, green, blue lights on the 'Ashoka stambha'. In front of the throne such a fountain had been made that sprays rosewater from its within. My heart lept from enthusiasm. I have rushed to you straight. You might have seen many tableaus, but this one is something very special. The world is pouring onto that. I have heard, some intelligent artisan has come from Delhi. This is his unique craft.

Unwillingly I said: I don't have the zeal to go there my friend, I have a severe headache.

—Then must you go, of course. See if your ache doesn't vanish forthwith?

—Oh my friend, you bother me so much. For this only I lay silently so to eschew such an irritation. I have already told you—I won't go.

—And I said already —I must take you along.

My friend keeps in his mind some very easy designs by which he can win over me. In scuffles, or brawls, or in fracas I never score behind anybody, but if someone titillates me, I get won over. At that condition I fail to have any say upon anybody. I begin appealing in folded hands, beg mercy of him or even start crying. Jaydev applied on me the typical trick and he won. For peace he advanced a condition that I must go to witness the *jhanki* without any further noise.

3

Seth Ghureylal was one of such humans, name whom in the morning you might even miss your day's meals. Hundreds of folk-tales about his parsimonious were talked about in the township. It's said that once a beggar from Marwar positioned himself with a resolve at his doorstep 'I would leave only after I'm given alms'. Sethji became adamant resolving too 'I won't give him alms at all, come what may'. The Marwari was from his own State. For some time he sang of his forbears, then spoke ill of them, and atleast lay down in the doorstep. Sethji did not care for him wee bit. The beggar too was rigid on his resoluteness. Whole day he lay there without food and water and at last there itself he expired. Only then melted Sethji who also performed the last rites of the man in such pomp and show that seldom anybody would have done any. He gave a feast to one lakh brahmins, and lakhs he paid in honorarium. The satyagraha of the beggar turned out to be a boon for Sethji. A current of devotion seemed to have unleashed in his heart. All his property he dedicated for religious purposes.

As we reached the Thakurdwara hundreds of viewers had already crowded the place. Shoulders rubbed against shoulders. Ways for entrance and exit were separated, and after an hour we got chance to enter. Jaydev was overwhelmed at the sight of decoration, but I was feeling that amidst this artificiality and show-off the soul of Lord Krishna was lost elsewhere. At the site of his gem-studded, electricity illumined idol I developed remorse in my heart. Well, could such idol house love in it? In gems reflected pretence and vanity. I did not keep in mind at that moment that, that was a temple by a millionaire, and the rich can only think of god who is decorated in wealth. Their reverence can only be restored on to wealthy gods. He who doesn't have wealth can only be fit to get their generosity, but never their reverence.

Jaydev was known to everybody in the temple. In fact, he was known to all at all the places. A music party was there at the courtyard of the temple. Hey, it was Kelkarji ensconced there with tanpura in company of his students of the Gandharva Vidyalaya! His students had with them pakhawaj, sitar, sarod, veena and many more instruments name of which I did not even know. One of the girl students was getting ready to play a cardinal musical note. Spotting Jaydev, Kelkarji called in forthwith. I also got seated in the party. Next moment the notes began. The gathering was spell-bound instantly.

At the place when a moment before was so much a din that even a canon fire would not have been heard, now a flow of beauteous melody absorbed in itself every heart present there. Whoever was there stood enchanted. Never was my imagination so picturesque, so lively. No longer in my vision was there the dazzles of electric lights, neither the glitters of gems, nor was the exhibition of those material shows-off. Instead, before my eyes appeared the same bank of Yamuna, shadowed under the veil of bushy creepers. The same beautiful cows flocking together, the water-game of the milk-maids, the honeyed wafting of tunes from the flute, the soothing moonlight and the same old dear Nandkishore, from the grace of whose face reflected glow of love and affection, at the sight of whom one's heart gets purified.

4

I was under the spell of such pleasant vision when her rendition came to its end and another disciple of Acharya Kelkar began singing a versified composition with remote details. It is the habit of these artists to twist and turn the verses in such manner that most of the listeners fail to make out what exactly they do sing. Not a word from the present lyric I understood; yet in his voice was some such captivating charm that each note of his was making me thrilled. Such profound magical power could be there in one's voice, I realised only today. In my heart a new world was being created when there was only ecstasy, love and the feel of renunciation. I felt that 'misery is but a function of mind, truth is only pleasure'. A clean merciful tenderness, as if, began to subdue my personal emotional upsurge. A feeling emanated from within me that every good fellow seated there was my own, inseparable part. And promptly emerged from the core of my past life my brother's image.

Many days since, my younger brother had fled to Rangoon after having quarrelled with me and grabbing family's accumulated wealth, and there itself his life came to an end. Recollecting his savage behaviour I used to get furious. Had I got him alive, perhaps I would have drunk his blood, but at this moment having seen his image in my vision my heart as if got filled with delight. I became eager to hold him in embrace. I forgot all the rude, mean and hateful behaviours which he did with me, my wife, with mother and my children. In my heart only one thought rang—'how unhappy is my brother'. Never before had I developed such feeling of kinship with this brother of mine but now my mind reached a stage which could be called bewilderment.

The feeling of animosity seemed to have wiped out of my heart. The people with whom I had the feeling of adversary, with whom I had exchanged abuses, beatings, litigation et al, they all seemed laughing in merriment in my embraces. Next moment image of Vidya, my wife, appeared before my eyes—the image of hers that I had seen ten years ago—in her eyes were the same restless quivering, same sceptic faith, in her cheeks were the same reddish glows of blush, as if a lotus flowered out of the pond of love. The same love of hers, the same intense emotion, the similar appealing anxiety wanned up by which during that unforgettable night I had welcomed her to my life—once again floated up in my heart. A stream of honeyed memories seemed to have flowed in me. My heart got so much elated that I felt I should forthwith go to Vidya, and weep rubbing my head against her feet and go senseless weeping. My eyes got tearful. Whatever rude words had come out of my mouth they seemed cutting into my own heart. Amidst this plight of mind, as if my loving mother emerged and lifted my tormented head into her lap. The ecstasy, which I had no power to derive from my mother's affection when I was child, I realised today.

The concert came to an end. All began rising to leave. I remained seated drowned in the sea of fancy.

Suddenly Jaydev called out: 'Will you now come or keep on seated there?'

❒

6. GULLI-DANDA

Our English friend likes it or does not I would say that gulli-danda is the king of all games. Even today when I see boys play gulli-danda, my heart rolls around dancing to play with them. No need of a sprawling lawn, nor of court, or net, or of a mallet. Gladly you cut a twig out of a tree, pare that to carve out a gulli, and also let there be two persons, the game is begun.

The greatest demerit in foreign sports is their equipments are dear. Until at least one hundred rupees are contributed a player cannot be taken into account. But here we have gulli-danda in which you invest nothing but gain everything. Yet we are so mad after English goods that we have developed aversion towards everything ours, indigenous. In schools, they take three or four rupees towards sports fees annually, but it never dawned on anybody that Indian sports be played; for the games can be played without cost of a farthing. English sports are for those who have wealth. Why do you impose such a luxury upon poor children? Okay, you fear that one's eyes might be pierced by gulli. But is not one afraid of getting his head split or his spleen torn or his legs broken by the cricket ball? Well, if even today there is a scar mark on my head caused by the gulli, then mind you, I too have many friends who take seat by the help of a mallet using as a crutch. It's one's personal taste. I consider gulli the best of all the games; and among the sweet memoirs of childhood, the gulli is the most honeyed.

The nostalgia of slipping out of home at the dawn, cutting of twigs by climbing atop a tree, to pare and carve out gulli-danda, well, the zeal and commitment whereby there cannot be any sense of difference like touchability or non-touchability or rich or poor, show-biz or vanity—all these one would forget only when yoked in harness of the game. Amid the anger of folks at home, expressed as one's dear father giving vent to his disapproval by hurried chewing up of his morning *chapatis,* when the dear mother anxiously rushing to and fro only upto the doorstep, though in whose toiled understanding my bleak future was seeming a tossed boat on the verge of tumbling; while me, away on the other hand, lost in the field carefree, devoid of the feel for bathing or fooding. Tiny is the gulli, yet contained in it is the sweetness of the entire world and frolics of all funs.

There was a boy named Gaya in my company. He might be two-three years older than me. A lean tall fellow with longish thin fingers like a monkey, behaving with the same monkeylike fickleness and tantrums. Whatever be the type of gulli, he used to fall upon it in such manner, as the lizard would jump upon insects. I did not know if his parents were living, or where he used to stay or eat; but he was our champion in the gulli-danda club. To whatever side he would fall-in, that side was sure to taste victory. If we had spotted him passing from a distance, we used to rush to welcome him and make a member in a side.

One day myself and Gaya—we two were only playing. He was pushing and I was fielding; but it is peculiar that whole day we can be yoked in pushing to field, yet fielding for others even for a minute might pinch. To eschew my turn of fielding I played all trickeries, which given in such occasions were pardonable despite their not being customary, but Gaya would not spare me without taking his turn completely.

I rushed toward my home. Appeals and argument had no effect on him.

With a smart run Gaya caught hold of me and brandishing his danda he said: You can go, only after fielding for my turn. You made me field for you and tired me as if you were a hero, and now when your turn for fielding came, why run away from it?

—If the whole day you continue to push, then should I have to field?

—Yes, the whole day you will have to field until I'm out.

—I won't go even for my food and drink?

—Yes, without completing my turn you cannot go anywhere.

—Am I your servant?

—Yes, you are my servant.

—I'm going home. Now let me see what you can dare to do.

—How can you manage to go your home? Is it a joke? I've fielded for you, now I would take your labour fielding for me.

—Okay, yesterday I had given you a guava, now you return that.

—That's gone into my stomach.

—Bring that out of your stomach. Why have you eaten my guava?

—The guava you only gave me, after that I had eaten it. I didn't come to beg for it?

—Until you don't return my guava, well, I won't field for you.

I had been thinking justice is on my side. After all, it was on some interest that I had given him guava to eat. Who treats one without some interest? Even giving some alms is also on some interest? Once Gaya had consumed my guava, he had forfeited his right of asking me to field for him. Well, people even digest blood having once palming in grafts. And this fellow would consume my guava just like that for nothing in return? That guava was of the quality that you get only five for a pice, which even Gaya's father must not have eaten in his lifetime. Hence, his was an outrageous injustice.

Gaya pulled me toward himself and said—I don't give a dime for your guava or what. Withdraw only after you have fielded for me.

I had the strength of justice. He was boasting upon injustice. I wanted to move away by jerking myself off from his clutch. But he won't let me go. I hurled an abuse for him, he returned one even harder than mine, and not only the abuse, he also landed a slap. I bit him in his hand, and he banged his danda on my back. I began crying. That was a weapon which Gaya could not counter, he fled. Forthwith I wiped off my tears, ignored the strike of the danda and laughingly reached my home. I, a son of a thana in-charge, got beaten by a low-caste urchin, this was felt insulting even at that time; yet I did not complain to anybody.

2

One of those days my father got transferred from his posting. Delighted at the thought of seeing new environs I got so much swelled up at my heart that not wee bit dejection touched me on the ensuing estrangement from my companions. My dear father was unhappy. The new place of posting did not promise big income. My dear mother was unhappy too, everything here was quite cheap, besides she had developed homeliness with other women in the locality. But I was in the seventh heaven out of joy. I used to brag before companions: 'the houses there are not such we see here. There are buildings so high as if they commune with the sky. If an English teacher there beats a boy, he might even facc imprisonment.' The widened eyes of my friends and their wonder-struck looks were telling how far elevated have I gone in their views. Children have a power to transform falsity into reality, which we the elders, who turn a fact into fiction, can rarely understand. How greatly envious those poor chaps were getting of me! As it were, they were telling— 'you are deified, brother, adieu, alas, we have only to live here at this desolate village and here only to die.'

Twenty years have passed. I passed engineering, and one day while touring round the same district I arrived at the same village and put up at the dakbungalow. The very look of the village surged in my heart a feeling of sweet reminiscences of my boyhood so much that I picked up my walking stick and came out to have a round of the village. My eyes were yearning to see those play grounds of my childhood days like a thirsty pedestrian's, but save that familiar name, nothing else was familiar to me. There, where were ruins, was now erected strong-built houses. Where there used to be a banyan tree, existed now a beautiful garden. The entire area had undergone metamorphosis. If I had not known its name and location, then I could not have even recognised the place. The immortal memoirs of my childhood which I have fondly preserved were yearning, as if with open arms, to embrace my old companions; yet that world of mine had been transformed. I was longing to fall flat upon that earth, embrace it, cry and tell: "You've forgotten me! But behold, even today I yearn to see the same of your look.'

Suddenly in an open ground afar I spotted two-three boys playing gulli-danda. For a moment I totally forgot my own positions. I forgot that I am a highly placed officer, in European robes and style, well-guarded by those rights and airs.

I moved toward a boy and asked: Well, my boy, do you know a man named Gaya living here?

One of the boys assorted the gulli and danda and in a nervous overtone asked: Who Gaya? The very one, Gaya chamar?

Cursorily I said: Yes-yes, the same. There's one fellow named Gaya, right? Maybe it's he only.

—Yes, there is one man of course.

—Can you please call him for a while?

The boy went running and in a moment he was seen coming out with a five-hand tall black godly man. I could recognise him even from the distance. I longed to leap forward toward him and hold him in fast embrace, but I held myself with some forethought. I asked him: —Tell me Gaya, can you recognise me?

Gaya bowed down offering salam and replied:—Yes my lord, well, how cannot I recognise you? Were you happy all these days?

—Yes, very much happy. Tell me how about you?

—I'm the syce at the deputy sahib's.

—Where are Matai, Mohan and Durga? Any news of them?

—Matai has died, Durga and Mohan both have become postmen. What about you sir?

—I am the district engineer.

—Well sir, you had been very sharp even in earlier days.

—Nowadays do you play gulli-danda at all?

Gaya looked at me with questioning eyes and said: How can I now play gulli-danda sir, I don't get anytime off from duties.

—Come, we two would play today. You'd push the gulli and I would field for you. I have one turn fallen due to you. Take that today.

After quite persuasion Gaya agreed. Well, he was an inconsequential workman whereas I a highly placed officer. How can we unite? The poor chap was blushing. But even I was not feeling ashamed any less. Not because I was going to play with Gaya, but because people would take this contest as peculiar and make a fun of it and there would be quite a crowd thronging around. Where would remain that pleasure? Yet, I could not afford to live in those hours without a game. At last it was decided that both of us would go far away at a solitary place and play there. Well, who can be there to witness our tie? We would play with our heart's fill and would return having drunk the nectar of honeyed childhood.

I came to dakbungalow taking Gaya in my company, and having ensconced in the motor-car we two moved towards the ground. Along with me I also took an axe. I was serious but Gaya was still taking it as a joke. Even then there was no sign of eagerness or happiness on his countenance. Perhaps he was lost in his consideration of the difference of status that has crept between us.

I asked: Did you ever have had thoughts about us, Gaya? Tell me the truth.

With a blush Gaya replied: Me? To think of you? Well sir, am I fit for that? It was luck by chance that I ever played with you, only for some days, where was I to be considered?

I said somewhat pensively: But always I had been thinking of you? That danda of yours which you had brandished and hit me with, you remember? No?

Repenting Gaya said: That was childishness my lord! Please don't remind me of that.

—Excellent! That was the juiciest memory of my boyhood. In that danda of yours was such a juicy thing, that I do not get from all the cares and honour now, neither in all the wealth I have! There was some pleasant thing in that which even today has been sweetening my heart.

By that time we came some three miles afar off the locality. It was solitude all round. In the west, for many *kos* was stretched the gigantic pond, from where once upon a time we used to pluck out lotuses and carving pendants out of them we used to fix them on our ears. Mixed with fragrance of *kesar* was wafting in the evening of *jaitth.* With a spring I climbed atop a tree and cut a twig from it. Forthwith were made gulli and danda. Our game started. I put the gulli into the pit and tossed it by help of danda. The gulli slipped away through Gaya's front. He flung his hand to catch hold of it, as if he was fishing it out of water. The gulli stopped behind him. It was same Gaya in whose hands the gulli used to pit, as it were, by itself. Wherever would he had been, left or right, the gulli used to land only into his palms. As if he had been mesmerising the gullis. Were it a new gulli, old gulli, small gulli, big gulli, pointed gulli or an even gulli—all used to come into his hands. As if there was a magnet in his palm, which promptly attracted the moving gullis. But today the gulli did not retain that loyalty for him. Hence thereafter I began hitting at the gulli ferociously. I used many types of trickeries. The loss of practice I was manipulating by cheating. Even when the gulli had been striking the danda, I went on playing the danda, whereas, actually, turn should have gone to Gaya. On the gulli my hits were mild and as that would drop nearby, I was leaping onto it to pick and hit second time. Gaya was witnessing all these irregularities; but nothing he spoke, as if he had forgotten all rules and regulations. And what an infallible aim he had! Once released from his hand the gulli used to come onto the danda with a bang. Having been thrown, its job seemed to be only to strike the danda. But today the gulli won't touch the danda by any means. Sometimes it would drop right of it, sometimes on its left, at times short of it and the next moment just behind.

It was half an-hour after constant hits, the gulli struck the danda. I played tricks arguing: The gulli hasn't touched the danda though it passed by brushing it; it did not touch it at all. Gaya did not express wee-bit dissatisfaction.

—Maybe it didn't touch.

—Had it touched so, well would have I cheated you?

—Oh no, *bhaiya*; well why would you cheat me anyway?

Now even this happening in the childhood could I ever dare to win by trickeries: This very Gaya would have been upon my shoulders imposingly; but today how easily I was pipping him off just by cheating. He was a donkey. Everything he seemed to have forgotten.

Suddenly the gulli struck the danda at one moment, and with such force as if a gun was fired. On a proof such as was that, I did not dare to do any trickery even at that time; but then, why not try once again to call everything as wrong? What had I to lose thereby? If he agreed, well it was excellent, if not I was only to field for two-three flings from Gaya. Thereafter I might get rid of him arguing darkness falling. And after that who would come here again to field for him?

With a hurrah Gaya said: Hey, it has struck, it struck with a bang!

Trying to prove unaware of it I asked: Have you seen it bang. I did not?

—It banged sir, loud.

—Or has it banged against a stone?

It was wonder even for me! How at that hour such an argument got released from my mouth? Trying to tell that truth a falsity was like calling the day a night. Both of us had witnessed the gulli hit the danda with force: but lo and behold, Gaya accepted my argument:— Yes, it might have hit a stone. Had it struck the danda, then it would not have sounded so loud.

Once again I began to fling the gulli; but after having succeeded in such stark mischief, I felt pity on Gaya's artlessness; hence soon as the gulli hit the danda for the third time I posed broad-minded and decided to offer him his due. Gaya said: Today it is dark brother, keep it for tomorrow. I thought that 'tomorrow' we would get enough time, and who knew how long this chap would make me do fielding; so it would be wise to clear the deal right at that time.

—No, no, now it is quite lighted. You take your turn of pushing.

Gaya began his turn of pushing the gulli; but he showed he did not have any practice of the game. Twice he tried to fling it hard, but twice he failed and missed out. By less than a minute he completed his turn. The poor chap had fielded for me for hours; but within a minute itself he lost his chance. I offered to prove munificence of my heart.

—Try to play another turn. Well, you missed your hand at the very first instance.

—No bhaiya, now it's quite dark.

—You seem to have lost your touch. Don't you play nowadays at all?

—Where to get time for games, *bhaiya*?

Both of us went back to the motor-car and got seated; by the time it was hour when homes were being illumined, we reached the locality. While leaving Gaya said: Tomorrow there would be contest of the gulli- danda games here. All the old stalwarts would come to join the match. Would you like to come? When you have the sparable time, tell me that, I would call people only at that hour.

The hour I fixed was the twilight. And the following day I went to witness the tie. Teams of ten heads each were there. Some were found to be my childhood companion there: Most of them were youth whom I could not recognise. The game started. Seated on my motor-car I witnessed the funs and frolicking. Today I witnessed Gaya's dexterity at the game which surprised me. When he pushed the gulli it communed with the sky. The hitches which he showed he had yesterday, the shilly-shally, and that lifelessness, were nowhere to be seen. The childishness which he showed yesterday attained maturity today. Had he made me field like he was doing others today, I would surely have broken down to weep. Having been hit by his danda the gulli was taking stock of two hundred yards forthwith.

Among the fielders one youth did some cheating. According to his view he had lept to catch the gulli. But Gaya was telling—the gulli had touched earth and then only bounced back upwards to him. On this, both came on the verge of a brawl. The youth got subdued; but to the angry countenance of Gaya he had to cow down. Had he not gone subdued, then surely there would have been a scuffle.

I was not within the game; yet from the games others were playing I derived the same ecstasy of childhood when we used to forget everything while playing it intently. Now only I realised that Gaya actually did not play with me yesterday, he in fact posed to play. He actually took me fit for pity only. I had tricked against him, I cheated him, but he did not get angry, in the least. It was because he was not playing the game, he was helping me play it, he was keeping up my spirit. He did not want to crush me by compelling me to field for him. I am now an officer. That personality of mine had stood like a wall between me and him. I can get honour from him, also the well-mannered etiquette, but not his companionship. When we were in our adolescence I was his equal. There was no divide between us. With my present position I am only fit for his kindness. No longer did he consider me his partner. He had become bigger than me in esteem, and I had become smaller.

❒

7. THE LIGHT
(Jyoti)

After she became a widow, Booti's nature had turned rudish. At every instance of her unbearable heart-burn, she used to implicate her dead husband. 'You departed but left behind all these trash for me to meddle with. I wonder why at all you married me, if you had the design to expire so early! You were poor as is a church mouse, yet you braved up to marry very well.' If she had desired she could have got engaged for the second time. Among Ahirs such is the custom. She was not disagreeable in her looks and bearings. As many as two grooms were even ready for betrothal, but Booti failed to drop the temptation of being called a virtuous widow. And she used to give vent to her frustration and anger on her eledest son Mohan, who was sixteen years old. Sohan was young then and Maina was her only daughter. Both of them were not competent to do anything. Had she not felt responsibility for these three children, then Booti never could have faced so much of adversity. Whomever she would have worked for, he would have given her food and clothings. She would have lodged her stake with anybody as she might have wished. Now if she abandoned these children and lived with somebody else, people would have wondered: 'she has three children, then what is this that fell upon her mind.'

Mohan laboured with all his might to reduce her workload. Feeding the cows and buffaloes, milking them, churn their output—all he used to manage by himself, yet Booti would not be satisfied. Every day she would somehow find some flaws in his works and by and by Mohan stopped paying any heed to her rebuffs. Her husband had left her in the lurch with entire load of household domesticities upon her shoulders was all her complaints. The poor woman thought herself ruined. She did not relish her food, neither feel happy in dressing herself, nor would enjoy any discourses. The lot that had befallen upon her family proved to have thrown it, as it were, into fire. Within her was going on incessant conflict between the custom-ordained penance from widowhood and insatiable yearn for sensual and earthly pleasures, in the fire of which all her gentleness was burnt off into ashes. Owing to her husband, Booti had ornaments worth at least four- five hundred rupees, but all were liquidated from her reserves one by one.

In the same locality among her fraternity were many women, who, even though they were seniors to her, were wives of her brothers-in-law in the fraternity, used to wander around upon her face with show-off and tinkles of their ornaments, their eyes decorated with collyrium, and parting lines on their heads heavily coloured by vermillion, as if, they wished to torment her. Booti, therefore, as and whenever someone of them was widowed, used to feel glad; but presently all her heart-burn she would avenge on her children, in particular upon Mohan. Perhaps she wanted to see all the women of the world at her plight. In rumour-mongering she used to derive special joy. Her thirsty sensuality, it seemed, having failed to burn off to satiety, derived contentment by sucking only the dew drops. Hence, how could it be a probability that she would hear anything about Mohan and suppress it after that to herself? Soon as Mohan returned home after selling off the day's milk, Booti asked: I find nowadays, you are out to become a wandering bull?

With questions in his eyes Mohan asked: What bull? What's the matter?

—Well, were you not bantering with Rupiya in the sly? Top of that you dare to ask what the bull is? Don't you be ashamed?

Here in the household we have acute stringency, and then you go to her with betel-leaves and get her saree dyed?

Mohan spoke revoltingly: If she would ask for betel worth a few pice what else should I had done? Should I have asked her 'get me the pice then only I'd fetch it for you'? She gave me her saree to get dyed, well, should I have asked her for its payment?

—Perhaps you are the only Dhannaseth in the locality. Why did not she ask somebody else for these?

—That she only knows, how could I tell you?

—Now you, it seems, are trying to become a dandy. Have you ever brought home betel even worth a pice?

—For whom should I have had brought betel-leaves home?

—What! All the members at home were dead for you?

— I did not know that you ever wanted to eat betel-leaves.

—Why? Of all people on earth only Rupiya was fit to eat betel-leaves, right?

—One may also have desires for funs and making oneself up.

Booti flared up. Implying her an old woman meant bogging all her youthful devotion. 'What is the utility in such spirited dedication in one's old age'—it was a hard blow upon her concept of selflessness by the strength of which she used to move strutting proudly. And she put dirt to all her youth working for these children. Five years were spent after the death of her husband. Hers was burgeoning youth at that time. God had flung three children around her neck, and what is her age now? If she desires even today she could move around with reddened lips, having decorated her feet with *mahawar*, putting on blinkers or *bichhiya*. She forsook all those things for these children, and today Mohan tries to call her an old woman. If Rupiya is placed beside her, she would look insignificant like a rat. Even after all this, that lass appears youthful to Mohan, and she is considered an old woman?

She replied: Oh, oh, yes. For me the time has come to put on tattered clothes like oldies, right? At that time of your father's death I was only two to four years older than Rupiya. Had I married to set up another household, none of you would have been traceable today. You would have loitered in lanes with begging bowls. But look here, if at all you are found chatting with her, that'll make end of your stay here, or mine.

Afraid Mohan replied: But I have already given her my word, mother?

—What kind of word?

—For engagement.

—If Rupiya enters my household, I'd flog her out with brooms. I think all this is her mother's tactics. That bawd seems plucking my son away from me. Even the smallest happiness of mine, the widow, cannot stand! They want to turn my son alien and thrust him onto my chest.

Shocked at this Mohan said: Mother, stop it, for God's sake. Don't spoil your own ground. I was thinking after a few days Maina would return to her house, and you would be left to yourself. That's why I was thinking to bring her our home. If that's bad to your eyes then, alright I'd drop the idea.

— From tonight you would sleep at the courtyard only.

—And the cattle would remain outside, unguarded?

—Let them remain so. They are not going to be raided by dacoits.

—But are you so much suspicious about me?

—Yes, I am.

—Well then, take it that I'll not sleep here.

—Then go away from my house.

—Yes, if that's what you want, I would.

Maina had cooked the meals, Mohan said: 1 don't have appetite for food. Booti did not come to appease him.

The adolescent heart of Mohan cannot anyhow acquiesce in his mother's rigid rules. If it was her house, let her be happy with it. As for himself he would find out some other shelter. In his rugged lifestyle Rupiya had filled in saps of sweetness. When he used to feel his life has become forlorn, when at moments an unspelt yearn would throb his heart, Rupiya walked in there like early spring blossoming him. Mohan would taste new sweetness in his life. If he would be at some works, his mind would lodge in Rupiya's, he would think what might he present her that would please her. Now after what happened here, how could he muster a face to see her? Would he tell her, 'Mother has asked me not to see you?' It was only yesterday. Under the banyan tree both had funny talks. Mohan had said: 'How beautiful are you Rupa! Hundreds of suitors would come for your hand. And what would you find in my household?, And what Rupiya had replied on it was still ringing in his heart like a melodious tune: 'I want you Mohan, and only you. May you be a chowdhury of a pargana I only want that Mohan; or be you a daily wager I would continue to want that same Mohan.' Now should he go to same Rupiya to tell, 'From today I do not have any business with you?'

No, that's not possible. He would not care for home. With Rupiya he would stay separate from his mother's. If not at this locality, let it be somewhere else. Even at that hour Rupiya might have been awaiting him. How deliciously she does prepare the betel leaves! If mother comes to know that he had gone to Rupiya's house at night, might she even forsake her life, let her do so, if she would. Well, she would not sing her luck that she would get such a good daughter-in-law. Why would she feel so much jealous of Rupiya, none knows. Sometimes she asked for betel leaves, sometimes she made him get her saree dyed and put that on. That's all!

He heard tinkles of bangles. Rupiya was coming; yes, it's she. Rupiya stood near his head and said: Have you fallen asleep Mohan? For an hour since I was awaiting you. Why didn't you come?

Mohan kept lying pretending asleep. Rupiya pushed his head and said: Well, have you already gone asleep, Mohan? What a feel of fulfilment was in those soft fingers, who knows! All his being become passionate. His life as if wanted to jump out of the cage of the room only to drop resigned at the feet of Rupiya. She was as it were the goddess standing there to shower boons. As if the whole world was dancing. He felt like having lost his own body, and like a melodious note hugged in the lap of the universe, he was only dancing with her.

Rupiya asked again: Are you asleep already, my dear?

Mohan replied: Yes, I got some nap Rupa. But why have you come at this hour? Supposing mother finds us, she might even kill me.

—Why didn't you come today?

—Today I fought with mother.

—What was she telling?

—She was telling: 'Speak to Rupiya again, I'll forsake my life'.

—Didn't you ask, 'Why are you so much fretful at Rupiya?'

—Well, what to speak of her Rupa? She would not stand other eat and wear good. From now onwards perhaps I would have to keep away from you.

—My heart won't agree with that.

—If you tell that, then I've to elope with you.

—Only see me once a day. That is all. I won't ask for anything else.

—And what about mother's annoyance?

—That means, I now understand, you don't actually love me.

—If I could, I would have caged you in my heart.

Right at that moment there was rap-trap on the door, and promptly Rupiya jumped away to flee.

2

Next day as Mohan got up from his bed his heart was filled with boundless joy. He was in the habit of nagging after Sohan ever always. Sohan was indolent. Never would he set his mind at household chores. Presently, in the morning was he slowly applying soap on his loincloth. Soon as he saw Mohan he got trying to find an excuse to move away.

Amusingly Mohan said: Your loin-cloth got dirty, right Sohan? Why don't you give it to the washerman?

In such words Sohan felt of affection.

—The washerman would ask for money.

—Why didn't you take it from mother?

—Mother won't pay the money.

—Then, take it from me.

Saying this he flung a one-anna coin to his direction. Sohan became pleased. Both his brother and mother hoot him generally. Long after he tasted any candid affection from somebody. He picked up the one-anna coin, left his cloth there itself, untied the cow from its stake and moved out.

Mohan said: Leave it, I'd take her out right away.

Sohan handed the tether to his brother and asked: Shall I make a *chhelum* for you?

First time in his life Sohan experienced his good feeling toward his brother. What was the riddle behind it Mohan could not understand. He replied: Alright, keep it, if you get some cinder.

Maina was busy in making a toy-house, her hairs untied and flowing. Soon as she spotted Mohan she broke away the toy-house she had already made. Then, while trying to conceal her disorganised flowing locks from Mohan's sight, she moved toward the kitchen to assemble utensils.

Mohan asked: What have you been playing, Maina?

Scared, Maina replied: Nothing particular.

— I find you can make very good toy-houses! Try again; I would like to see that.

Maina felt spirited, as she shook off the fear. What a magic is there in loving words! As if, they spread incense soon as they are out of one's lips. Having heard him her heart lept up. Trust took over the place where was fear only. Feelings of owning spilt forth in place of rudeness. A streak of awareness diffused itself all around. No more lethargy, no more hopelessness. Mohan's heart was full of love today. Incense wafting out of it.

Maina set down to build the toy-house once again. Mohan wanted to appease those who was feeling aversion toward him. Tell me Maina, when are you going to marry off your doll? Will you invite me? I'll get some chance to eat some sweets that day?

Maina's heart began flying over the sky. From now on whenever *bhaiya* would ask for drinking water, she would wash the lota shining by rubbing ashes on it repeatedly.

—Mother doesn't give money to celebrate the wedding. The groom-doll has been chosen. How would I send the teeka?

—How much do you want for that?

—Well, *batasa* for one pice and vermilion for another pice. The loin-cloth and the scarf have to be dyed, after all?

—By two pice all your requirement would be fulfilled!

—Oh yes, brother, give me only two pice please, I can manage the wedding of my doll with pomp and show?

Mohan took out two coins and put them onto his own palm in full gaze of Maina. Amused, Maina lept for them, but forthwith Mohan lifted his palm high beyond her reach; Maina hung from his arm trying to pull his palm down. Affectionately, Mohan lifted her altogether to his lap. Maina took the coins out of his palm, climbed down and began dancing, overjoyed. Thereafter she ran away to invite her friends to the marriage ceremony.

At that time Booti showed up carrying the basket full of cattle-dung. Having spotted Mohan standing idly she charged:

Well, you are still fiddling around? When are you going to milk the buffaloes?

Today Mohan did not counter Booti with a retort. A flood of euphoria seemed unleashed in his heart. Seeing his mother with the burden of accumulated dung he moved forward and pulled the burden down from her head.

Booti said: Leave this, I say, go and milk the buffaloes. I can carry away the dung very well.

—Why do you lift such heavy burden always? Why didn't you ask me for it?

The mother's heart got filled with affection for her son.

—You better go and look after your jobs. Don't bother about me.

—Listen, assorting about the dung is my work, not yours.

—And who's to milk the buffaloes?

—That too is my job.

—Are you such a hero that all these you would be able to manage?

—I'll be able to do what I say.

—Then what am I to do?

—Why? You only take the works from your sons, that which is ordained by nature?

—Well, does anybody care for my talks here?

3

As Mohan returned today from the market after having distributed the milk, he brought with him betel-leaves, catechu, betel-nut, one small betel-container and some sweets. Annoyed at this extravagance Booti asked him: Why? Have you made some extra bucks today? How long would we be able to pull on if you squander away money like this?

—But I haven't squandered a farthing mother! Earlier, I only thought that you never eat betels, that's all.

—So? Today I have to eat them?

—Oh Yes! Why not? She, who have two youthful sons won't even feel like having fancy for good things in life? Even on such simple things?

At some nook of Booti's hardened heart emerged some verdant thoughts, some tender green saplings. Alas! what great liveliness she had in her heart, how full of saps. She gave Maina and Sohan a piece of sweetmeat each, and was about to give Mohan one, when he said: Sweets I have brought for my younger ones, mother.

—Why? Do you think you're grown up now?

—In presence of them surely I'm old.

—But to me you are only a child!

Mohan accepted the sweetmeat. Maina had almost gulped the sweetmeat soon as she had it, and was left only with the taste of sweetness in her tongue. Presently she was greedily looking at Mohan's share. Mohan halved his piece of laddoo and gave that to Maina. One piece was now left in the *dona.* Booti held it forward to Mohan telling: You brought only so little of sweetmeat.

Mohan put the halved piece into his mouth replying: That's your share, mother.

— I get much more sweet taste in seeing you all eat. She halved the lone sweetmeat and gave one half to Sohan and the other to Mohan. Then she opened the betel-box and looked into it. For the first time in her life today she met with such good luck. Blessed was she, as she attained the majestic position during her son's time, which she had been longing to get so ardently when her husband was alive.

There are many slots in the betel-box. Low and behold, there are two tiny pipes too; on top of the lid there was a metal ring, you carry the box wherever you want. In the upper tray betel-leaves are to be kept.

Soon as Mohan went out, she washed the betel-box clean, put lime into that, catechu, pieced some betels nuts, then kept the whole leaves watered. She folded a betel leaf to make one and ate that. The vegetated sap from it almost soothed her rude arid widowhood. Munificence of human heart practically is expressed in broad-mindedness. Now she could not remain confined within her four walls. Her heart was not deep so much that such an attainment in her life could be concealed to vanish into it. There was an old mirror. She saw her face into it. Her lips had been reddened, by the saps of it.

At that time came Dhania, and asked: Aunt, give me some rope; mine has broken.

Had it been even yesterday, Booti would have replied bluntly: My rope is not meant for all in the village. If the rope is broken, go and better get it remade. But today she pulled out her rope and gladly gave it away while asking: How is your son Dhania? Is his dysentery controlled or not?

Sadly Dhania replied: No aunt, the whole day he had it. Perhaps it's the teething trouble for him.

—Well then, let me come with you after you have fetched water, and would see for myself what is the matter. Is it the teething trouble or some other problem? Are you sure, nobody had cast an evil eye upon the child?

—Who can guess about that, aunt? Who knows if anybody has cast an evil look at him?

—Attractive children are feared to fall prey to evil looks much quickly.

—Well, whoever calls him carressingly, forthwith he jumps into her lap. Thereafter he gives some very lively laughs, which is beyond any description.

—Sometimes even mother's gaze has the untoward effects.

—Oh, my aunt, well, can one do evil things to her own child?

—This is what you would never realise. Evil falls upon child unaware.

Soon as Dhania returned having fetched water, Booti accompanied her to see her child.

—You're alone, you must be facing difficulties in managing your household chores.

—No aunt, Rupiya comes here every day, clears up some of my household jobs. Otherwise I would have died perhaps doing all these on my own.

Booti was surprised. She had taken Rupiya only as a glamorous girl. She asked in total surprise: What Rupiya?

—Yes aunt. The poor girl is very simple. She sweeps, clears up kitchen works, upkeeps the child. Who cares to think for others at the time of crisis?

—Well, she must not be getting time from make-up.

—Well, this of course is an individual's like or dislike. No affectionate person has given me help as much as did this make-up woman, as you call her. The poor soul had remained awakened nights after nights. Never I repaid her in any way. But yes, I would sing her praise as long as I would live.

—But you are not aware of all her great deeds, Dhania. You don't know how she manages to get money for her daily quota of betels or from where does she get her embroidered sarees.

—I don't want to get involved in such gossips. However who does not enjoy to make herself up? After all this is the time for a young maid to eat well and wear good.

They arrived at Dhania's house. In the courtyard was seated Rupiya patting the child to sleep on her lap. The child has fallen asleep by now.

Dhania picked the child up from her lap and placed him onto the craddle. Booti felt his head by her carressing palm, examined his belly by pressing slowly upon it. She advised to apply paste of asafoetida. Promptly Rupiya brought a hand-fan and began fanning with that.

Booti asked: Give that to me Dhania.

—If I do the fanning for a while that won't reduce my esteem.

—All the day you work here. You must have become tired by now.

—Such a good person you are, and people here speak of you that you don't talk without abusing. I never go to see you just out of scare.

Booti smiled: People don't lie after all?

—Well, should I believe what I have seen with my own eyes, or what I have heard?

Today also Rupiya has applied collyrium, chewed betel, put on a dyed saree, but it is today only Booti realised that the flower, that she is, also has fragrance. The aversion that she had developed toward Rupiya washed away forthwith, as if, by the providence of some goddess. How well-mannered a lass is she, how bashful! How tender is her voice. The girls of today do not care even for their own children, what to think of looking after others! The whole night she kept herself awoken for Dhania's little son. Mohan must have told her of everything that happened yesterday at home. Had she been some other type, she would have turned her face away from me. Might have she mortified me, or might have behaved conceited. But this lass does not seem to be knowing anything, at all. Yes, that's the reason.

Booti found Rupiya very charming today. It's all right; if she does not make herself up now, as she might fancy at her age as this, when else she would do that? Ordinarily people are in the habit of casting aspersion on human tendency of wearing make-up or dressing, because these make one habituated in luxury and debauchery.

Such people do not care even if somebody's house near them is on fire. Their only concern is to captivate other. As if, they have decorated their shops, calling out to the passersby, 'Oh, come for a while, have a round in this shop too'. But dressing or make-up by a benevolent person like her do not bear ill-feeling.

No, instead they look rather better. This confirms that this lass has a beautiful heart much as she has her physical beauty; so who won't desire to show-off her beautiful look. Doesn't a woman rear the desire to get vanquished in one's admired gaze? Booti's youth was long wasted away; even now she feels the desire. When someone looks at her with desires how happy she becomes in her mind? She used to get puffed up, proud. Whereas Rupiya is only a young lass.

From that day on, once or twice daily Rupa would visit Booti's household. Booti prevailed upon Mohan to get a good saree for her. If Rupa used to come to her sometimes without applying collyrium or with colorless saree on, then Booti would suggest: Girls of the stature of a daughter-in-law or daughter do not look good in ascetic dresses. Such simple dresses are for old women as I am.

One day Rupa asked: Why do you think that you have gone old, mother? Give some indulgence and you would find people flocking at your door like black bees upon a flower.

Booti chided her indulgently: Hey well, I'd die a co-wife to your mother, right?

—My mother is already very old.

—Why then, is your father very young?

—Yes, he looks like that. He is brought up of good stuff.

Booti looked at her with a full admiring gaze and then asked: Now tell me should I get you married to Mohan?

Rupa blushed. Rosy tinge spread all through her face.

Today as Mohan returned after selling off his stock of milk, Booti said : Now Collect some money, I am negotiating your marriage with Rupa.

❒

8. THE QUEEN OF HEART
(Dil Ki Rani)

The lanes of Kustuntunia today are flooded by blood of Turk soldiers, the warriors whose fierce exploits had created tremors in Christian world. It is the same Kustuntunia which had been afflicted from the scare of the Turk warriors, and which however, today is cooling its heart with the still warm Turk blood. Lifeless bodies of seventy thousand Turks are floating in the waves of Busforus and the Turk commander-in-chief is standing in front of mighty Taimur, accompanied by his one lakh soldiers, awaiting sentences upon fates of his as well as his men.

Taimur lifted his conquer-haughty eyes at the commander Yajdani and roared like a lion: What do you expect? Life or death?

Yajdani raised his head up with undaunted pride and said: If it's honourable life, then give life, otherwise death.

Taimur's anger turned ferocious. He had pulled down heads of many a mighty warrior. Such an answer he never had the mind to even hear from anybody. These one lakh lives were at his disposal. In one moment he could crush all of them. Even upon such eventuality this is his audacity! What! a life of honour is his expectation! The only implication of such a choice can be— lives of the poor to be consigned for the luxury and debauchery of the rich lifestyle.

To allow to revive once again the same lifestyle of wine parties, the same Armenians and the bevy of beautiful dames. ... Oh no, not for this Taimur has crushed the vanity of Khalif Byzid, not just to re-enliven the Turks again and allow them continue their exploits out of power- blind concept of freedom and thereby tarnish the very name of Islam. Had he had decided so, what was the necessity in shedding so much of human blood? Stream of human blood is not like wafting of any music, nor even flow of just some kind of blood—it gives a terrible view, which turns away onlookers' sight; the spectacle bows down one's head in shame. Besides, Taimur was not a ferocious animal, that he would bet his own life to witness such heinous sight.

He mixed censure in his words to reply his captive —The life which you call honourable is but one of crime and hell.

Yajdani did not expect kindness or clemency from Taimur. His life or his warriors' could not be saved by any means. Why then should he be tamed? And why should he not belch out all his hatred for Taimur which would simply risk his doomed life? For once he cast a grief-stricken look at the handsome youngman standing just behind him, who as though was restraining the leash of his arrogant youth. There seemed sparklings of immeasurable anger reflected out of his limbs like whetted steel. Yajdani saw his stature and looked like pushing back his unsheathed sword in the sheath, thereby having suppressed his anger, he said: Jehanpanah, you are in triumphant mood now, if you pardon me then I'd say, the Turks won't need to take Tartarians' advice in matters relating to their lifestyle. Besides, where Khuda has showered divine blessings, it is one's thanklessness then not to enjoy those blessings. If swords were the testimonials of civilization then the race Gaul would have been much more civilized.

Taimur laughed aloud and his soldiers promptly put their hands on their swords. Taimur's explosion of laughter was like explosion of death or of falling thunder.

—Tartarians are animals? Right?

—I cannot tell that.

—You claim, Khuda has created you to enjoy the world. I call it blasphemy. Khuda has created humans for worshipping only and against His will whoever does anything he is a kafir, a condemned fellow. The Holy Child had appeared to make our life happy and pious, to make us honest humans, and not to train us into ungratefulness! Taimur has taken up this holy war to transform the blasphemy into piety. I swear by the steps of the Holy Son I'm not merciless, not a rogue, not even a ferocious terrible; yet punishment for blasphemy, according to my prestige is nothing but death.

He cast a murderous glance at the Tartarian *Sipahsalar,* and instantaneously one god-like man came almost upon Yajdani's head brandishing forth his sword. At the same moment the Tartarian soldiers unleashed their swords and pounced upon the Turks, and within the breathing time many bodies fell on grounds writhing in mortal wounds.

All of a sudden the same handsome youth, who was standing behind Yajdani moved forward in front of Taimur, violently closing his tied up fists as though he was squeezing death into it said: Oh the Badshah, who boasts himself a Mussalman, is it that Islam which you have undertaken to protect? This is the lesson you have taken from Islam that you heinously murder those heroes who did not do any crime save protecting their motherland?

Silence befell all around. A lone youngmart as was he, whose moustache was yet to appear, would dare to chide a valorous Badshah like Taimur, in such blatant words, and that brat's tongue would not be snatched uprooted from its palate? All became dumbfounded, sitting there Taimur was looking at his enchanted.

The youngman glanced at the Tartarian soldiers who were eyeing him with wonder and curiosity and then said: You call these Mussalmans kafir, and you are thinking that by slaughtering them you are only serving Khuda and Islam? I ask you, if these people, who don't do *sizda* before anybody but Khuda, who consider the Holy Prophet only their guide, are not Mussalman then who else are Mussalman? I tell you, we might be the *kafir*, but we are your people after all? Does Islam ordain to slaughter the captives who are in chains? If Khuda has blessed you with strength and right, then does it suit you of killing me who is only a servant of Khuda? Would you like to bring the erring people on the right path just by butchering them? How soullessly cruel were you when seventy thousand brave Turks you blew away through mines! Can you at all guess how many guileless children you orphaned and how many innocent wives you ruined by widowing? Well, are these the deeds upon which you claim yourself a Mussalman? Will you brightly write your name in history of world with blood spilt from such butcheries, wounds and tortures? Not merely have you soaked tails of your horses in flowing sea of Turk blood, you have only uprooted thereby and thrown away Islam. It was but valorous Turks' self-sacrifice which had unfurled the flag of Islam in Europe. Today in the Church of Sophia you can always hear Allahh- Akbar, as much as entire Europe is ready to welcome Islam. Are these the doings for their rewards? Remove from your heart the thoughts that you are actually serving Islam by swords. You also have to answer before the Almighty and not any of your excuses would then be heard; for, if you are still left with any decency and gentility, then ask your soul! Whether the *jehad,* that you think you have waged is for the path of Khuda or for satiety of your own passion; and I know the answer you'd get would pull your head down in shame.

His head bent down, the Khalif was silent, but Yajdani appealed to Taimur in a voice trembling in fear: Jehanpanah, he is the son of this servant of yours. He has crazy thoughts in his mind. Oh my lord, kindly pardon him for his impertinence. I offer myself to withstand punishment for his impudence.

Taimur stared at the countenance of the youth. It was first time that day he had occasion to face fearless talks. Powerful commanders, ministers, and Badshahs never dared to open their mouths in his presence. Whatever had he had said were the laws, none ever had the cheek to question in them. In fact it was such flatteries that uplifted his vanity to the seven skies. He had developed a conviction that Khuda had sent him on earth to rouse the Islam and do reforms. That self-assumption was deep-rooted in his heart, though he never claimed to have become a Paigambar; that's why his conscience got a kick up as the youngman flung open today his veil of glory! Feeling of veneration surged in him in place of anger and ferosity. Life of this youngman could have been extinguished by one indication from him. This know-nothing boy standing before his world-conquering power as if was trying to stop the terrible current of sea by his tiny hands. How ludicrous was his valour, yet how greatly self-confident. Taimur felt much powerless in presence of this armless boy. Their could be only one current of such dare-devil valour and that is non-challant faith in Truth. He felt that his soul had become impatient desirous of embracing that youngman. He was not a philosopher, who might doubt the reality. He was a simple soldier, who by dint of sheer conviction could turn even the untruth into truth.

In same anxiety-torn voice Yajdani repeated: Oh Jehapanah let not your excellency take notice of his ill-talks.

But Taimur rose up forthwith and embraced Yajdani, thereafter said: Alas, if I had any occasion before to listening to such impertinent and ill talks, then my shoulders would not have been burdened with the crimes of slaughtering of so many innocent people today. From his utterings I see sparklings of some divine spirit, which seems to have been sent to show the sinners, as I am, the righteous path of life. My friend, you are blessed with good luck that you are the father of such a righteous son. Well, may I ask his name?

Earlier Yajdani was an idol worshipper, later he became a Mussalman. Yet even now quite often he used to be haunted by doubts as to why he embraced Islam. A captive withering on the gaol out of agony about to get the noose on his neck by which he was to be hanged lifeless, as if, got a sudden embrace by a divine fairy. With emotion-choked voice he replied: His name is Habib.

Taimur moved himself in front of the youth, held his hand and touched with them his own eyes telling: My young friend, truly are you Habib of Khuda. I'm that offender who out of his boorishness considered all the crimes just. That's all because I was challengingly told Tou are born of a viceless tribe'. Today only I realised how grievously Islam is abused by me. From today only I would follow you. You're my coach, you are my guide. I'm convinced, by the help of your guidance only I will be able to reach the *dargah* of Khuda.

While telling so he cast a glance at the feature of the youngman, and found it reddened with shame. Sweet bashfulness was streaked there in place of its earlier rudeness.

With his head bent down he replied: It's only greatness of your excellency, or which mettle have I owned?

Taimur escorted him to have a seat beside his own, and ordered his commander-in-chief to free all the Turk soldiers, return their weapons and distribute among them equally all the looted articles.

As his Wazir began working to fulfill the order, Taimur took Habib to his own camp holding his hand by his, and ordered for a feast for the two guests. When the feast was over, with tearful eyes he narrated all the stories of his own life, which from its beginning to end was full of misdeeds of his animal instinct and barbarity. Those days he was under the conceited belief that all that he was doing was only obeying of the Almighty's wishes. Now, how could he face Khuda? His laments became passionate enough to give him hiccups.

At length he said to Habib: My friend, you only could shore up the boat of burden. If you have shown me the path, then show me the destination as well. You only can reorganise my reign as Badshah, as I'm now convinced that my haughty pursuit was only leading me to afflictions. Now, my prayer to you is that—kindly accept my ministership. Oh behold for Khuda's sake, don't refuse, or I won't be saved from mortification by any means.

Yajdani appealed: Your excellency, it's your great patronage, it's your benevolence. However what's his age kindly consider. How would he manage to serve as a minister? His is only a training period now.

From one side was refusals, and from Taimur's came insistence. Yajdani was refusing to accept the offer, though his chest was being inflated with pride. Musa had only gone to collect fire, but achieved the status of Holy Spirit. They were going to embrace death, but ended up in achieving ministership; nevertheless were there anxiety and doubts—what was guarantee of such fickle-minded man? A fellow, who, if happy today, would offer ministership, but if unhappy tomorrow might even threaten life. He had faith in Habib's capability, yet his heart was scared at what might he come to face, and what not when he is in an alien land. In courts there are instances of rivalry and conspiracy, always. Though Habib is honest, understanding and able to test time; yet where was that experience of life which one gathers only with age.

To decide over this question, he begged one day's time and got relieved temporarily.

3

Habib was Yajdani's daughter and not a son. Her name was Ummatul Habib. Her age was only twelve when Yajdani and his wife embraced Islam; but along with intelligence and talent, nature has endowed her with competence of free thinking. She would not accept anything until she verified herself. Though she was unhappy at her parents' conversion, yet she could not do the same just for the sake of pleasing them, until of course she studied Islam herself thoroughly. Her parents also never wanted to exert any pressure onto her for the purpose. As it was their right to change their religion, so it was hers to remain in her religion she was born with. Their daughter developed faith in the religion; but thereafter she began comparative studies between Islam and Zarathustrianism and after two-year research and examination she got initiated in Islam. Her parents became overjoyed. Their daughter did not embrace Islam under their influence, but by her own will. The spell of anticipation which had engrossed them for two years was then quelled.

Yajdani had no son, and that at an era, when man's sword was the highest justice-giver, not having a son was considered very ill-fate. Yajdani realised in his daughter all his dreams about a son. She was given education and training like a boy, she would be dressed like a boy, ride on horses, learn how to use weapons and fight, and with her father quite often she visited Caliph Wayzid's palaces or used to go out for hunting accompanying the princess. At the same time she used to study philosophy, poetry, science, and also spiritualism so much so that at the age of sixteen she entered military academy and within two years she successfully cleared its highest examination to join services of the army. She became very deft in weaponry and commanding the army and Caliph Wayzid became so much happy with her character that in the very first instance she acquired commanding office incharge of one-thousand soldiers.

Could there be any want of lovers of such a young damsel. Many officers in her company, many youth from the royal family would love even to sacrifice their lives for her sake; yet none would go upto the esteem of her attraction. Almost every day would come offers of betrothal, but all she would turn down, always. She had aversion toward the married life itself. As she had freedom loving nature she did not want to be in such a bondage. Besides she used to observe regularly that young maids were married and brought homes in great expectations, yet with great disrespect they are confined within the palaces. Their wishes were dependent upon the males.

Often she had chances to mix up with women from highborn families. She came to know from them pathetic stories of their conjugal lives, which all the more convinced her to hate matrimonial bondage. And Yajdani also would never put hurdles in her freedom of mind. The daughter was free. Might she marry if she liked, or remained unmarried, all she would face by herself. Any proposal might come to him, but he used to reply in clear terms—"I don't know anything about such matter. She alone would decide about it.'

Though it was a point of discussion in the society as to how a young woman was okayed to dress like a young man, and freely mix up with them, yet both Yajdani and his wife had unflinching faith in her virginity. Never had they any doubt about it from demeanour of Habib. At twenty four she, a valourous young woman, remained unmoved amid dust-storm of youth and tempest of longings; as if all in the society were her own brothers.

4

These are no topics worth writing as how much was celebration in Kustuntunia, or how greatly was Habib honoured and welcomed, or how many greetings had she acquired. The township was on the brink of disaster. From all its houses and markets today, probably, might have emerged flames of fire, engulfing it. The person who saved the state and the township from such unimaginable disaster, should become a recipient of what degree of honour, love, regards and a source of how heartfelt joy— that's not even thinkable. May be a poet can visualize how much flowers and red jewels were showered on her; besides, women of the township were offering her from their heart their everlasting store of blessings and were feeling blessed themselves thereby at the sight of her proud elated face. She had uplifted the esteem of all the women.

At night began discussion over Taimur's proposal. Over a cushioned chair, presently, was seated Yajdani— amiable, great and imposing. On his right was his wife in her Irani attire, kindness in her eyes and bright with confidence. On his left was Ummutul Habib, who presently was in her woman's dress, attractive, glowing with the power of celibacy.

Opposing the proposal Yajdani said: I don't want to tell anything from my own but if you consider I have rights to advise you, then may I tell you clearly that you should not accede to such proposal. It cannot be concealed from Taimur for long as to what in reality you are. What would be the situation at that hour, I don't know but the comments that would rent the air here, you are aware of that more than I'm. Here I was present, so I didn't allow scandalous talks open, but there you would remain alone, scandalous rumours would have enough scope to float.

His wife would not like to give much importance to her self-will. She said: I have heard that Taimur does not look decently at women. I won't allow you go there by any means. If anything happens, then the world would laugh at us. Not a lesser number of people laughing at us already here?

The wife and the man continued similarly expressing their varied anxieties but Habib kept seated, silent. Yajdani thought Habib too was agreeable with them. They were about to send the message of their refusal, when Habib said: What are you going to tell Taimur?

—Only what we decided just now.

—But I didn't tell anything as yet?

—I thought you also are agreeable with us?

—No sir! Kindly tell him that I accept the offer.

Her mother placed her hands on her own bosom telling: What the hell you are out to do my child? Think for a while what the world would say of it?

Yajdani sat down dejected, pressing his head by hands, as if he had received a fire at his heart. Not a word came out from his mouth.

With wrinkles drawn upon her forehead she said: My dear mother, I would never like to turn away from your order. You have absolute right to allow me go or not to go there. But an opportunity such as this, serving the earth, perhaps I would never get all my life again. Allowing such an opportunity slip away from my grip might make me lament all my life. I am convinced that by the strength of my truthfulness, selflessness and accurate faithfulness I would be able to transform the barbarous Taimur into an honest human and perhaps never again blood of servants of Khuda would be shedded by his ruthless hands. He is daring but not merciless. In fact a daring man cannot become merciless. Whatever misdeed he did so far all were out of passion of the faith. Khuda has ordained me a chance that I can teach him that religion is the name of service to mankind and not of murder. As for myself, I don't have the least misgivings. I can look after myself. I have the confidence that fulfilling my duties in righteous manners I would even be able to silence my adversaries; even then consider for a moment, if I fail in my mission, is it not the brilliant victory of life to sacrifice itself for truth and rights? The principles with which I have spent my life so far, never betrayed me, and it is owing to that strength I have attained this status in life which actually are dreams of many mighty personalities.

Such time-tested friend that I have within me can never fail me. Besides, what is the scare if my real personality comes open before Taimur? My sword can protect me. As for marriage, you are aware of my views. If I find a man whom my soul can accept, with whose individuality I might love to unite my being and thereby uplift my soul, I would rather submit myself falling down upon his feet.

Yajdani became happy and embraced his daughter. But his wife was not convinced so easily. Never anyhow would she allow her daughter go there alone. She decided to accompany her.

5

Many months passed away. Young Habib was then minister at Taimur's; but in reality she was acting as the Badshah. Taimur used to see through her eyes, listen through her ears, and think at the level of her wavelength. He wanted Habib stay around him whole day every day. At her company he used to attain heavenly pleasure. And there was nobody in the entire Samarkhand who might feel envious of her. By her behaviour she had enchanted every body because not a bit ever she flinched away from justice. Even those who might be crushed under the weight of justice at her aegis, would also keep good relations with her, more or less, for never she used to make reins of justice go bitter more than necessary.

It was dark already. Royal employees had left for the day. Wax candles were burning at the lampstand. Entire court-hall was filled with fragrance from incense. As Habib was about to leave too, a watchman came to announce: Huzoor, Jehanpanah is coming.

This did not make Habib much happy. Like other ministers she never hankered after Taimur's company. Always she used to keep distance from Taimur. Rarely it ever happened when she took her meal in the royal dining room. Even get-together parties thrown by Taimur she never attended. Every day in the solitary as she narrated her day-long activities and experience and as thereafter his mother used to stamp her approval onto them, she used to attain peace.

He welcomed Taimur at the door. While seated himself on the throne Taimur said: I became surprised Habib, how you spend your such youthful life like Zahid. Khuda has endowed you with such handsome features that pretty, charming and even the most delicate beautiful damsels would feel fortunate to become your beloved. I do not know if you are aware of the news that, when you go out riding on your musky horse thousands of eyes eagerly await at windows all around Samarkhand, just to have a passing glance at you; yet nobody ever saw you lookup at any such direction. My Khuda is the witness how sincerely I long to toe in on your path. Alike you I too want to remain aloof from the world while living within this world. But I neither have that heart nor the brain. All the time I gnash at myself or at the whole world. All the time I feel thirsty, for blood from wars which you won't allow me to quench, and despite knowing fully well that whatever you do, none else would do that better, I cannot keep my anger within my check. You spread enlightenment and love wherever you pass through. Whoever could have been your foe, hence, becomes your friend. Whereas whichever way I pass through, I forge ahead spread-hatred and panic. He who's supposed to be my friend, becomes my enemy. In the whole world I have only this place, at yours, where I get my solace. If you consider this crown and the throne the obstacles in my path, then today itself I would kick these out. And presently I have come to you with this appeal that you show me that path from which I would be able to attain true happiness. I want, you to stay in the palace itself so that I can learn the lesson from you for righteous lifestyle.

Habib got a throb of awe. Was the secrecy about her womanhood broken to the ameen? For the moment she could not find out an answer. At such self-reproach of Taimur her heart melted. The mighty fellow on whose very reference the whole world acts awe-stricken was begging for enlightenment from her as a pitiable seeker. She saw a tender pleasant lustre in Taimur's expression, which otherwise was a rude, disfigured, harsh, violent stance, as if his awakened conscience was peeping from his within. Her steady lifestyle, wherein there was no sprightliness to rise any longer, seemed trivial before such fruitless enterprise.

In charmed overtone she said: Huzoor, you have such sincere care for a servant as I am, that's my fortune, yet it is not practicable for me to stay in the Shahi palace.

Taimur asked: Why?

—Because where there is plenty of money, dacoity takes place. Similarly where there is much care, there throng many enemies.

—Well, could there be any enemy of yours!

—I myself would turn out to be my own enemy. The most sworn enemy of a human is his vanity.

Taimur seemed to have found some jewels at this. He found some glimpse of self-contentment. He repeated to himself -'The most sworn enemy of a human is his vanity'. Then he said: I think Habib, never would you come within my reach. You are that bird which can soar only high in the sky, unreachable. Even confined in golden cage it would continue fluttering. However, Khuda Hafiz!

Forthwith he turned toward his shahi palace, as if the jewel he got he was eager to keep that securely. Never he had heard such a talk. But the knowledge, the instruction, the noble inspiration that he got today, he never had acquired before.

6

Rebellion was reported from areas of Istkhar. Habib became afraid that Taimur would rush there and effect a massacre.

He wanted to adopt peaceful methods to quell the rebellion and show thereby how powerful is the goodwill mission. Taimur on the other hand did not want to send her to do that arduous task; however, he yielded to Habib's insistence. When all her reasonings had failed then Habib said the last stake: As long as this humble servant of yours is present, your excellency, your jumping in an arduous risk, cannot be acceptable.

Taimur replied with a smile: Well Habib, as for my life it does not have more relevance than yours. Besides, never I cared for my life. What else I have left for the world to remind of me except massacres and loot? You can rest assured that in the event of my death, this world will not weep for me. A marauder like me will continue to be born always, but Khuda forbid, if anything untoward happens to you—ah! Let it happen to your enemies—this Sultanate would be razed to dust, then even I would have to be left with no other option but stabbing my chest with a sword. I cannot tell you Habib, how much have I gained from you. Alas! had I had secured your company ten-five years ago, then the history of Taimur definitely would not have been written with so much hatred. If it is so required today, I can sacrifice for you hundreds of Taimurs like me. You should realise that you take my soul away with you always. Today I tell you Habib, I have fallen in love with you, the love which I never felt for any beautiful girl. Now only I can realise what love actually is. But tell me what's the wrong there if I accompany you?

With her perplexed heart Habib said: If I feel your presence is necessary, I would inform you.

Stroking his beard Taimur replied: As you wish, but send a messenger every day, otherwise I might reach there out of anxiety.

With great love Taimur arranged for Habib's expedition. Various things were assorted for her comforts and formalities. In that barren land such things were not available. It was a moment, as it were, a mother was making arrangements to send her daughter to her in-laws.

At the hour when Habib left along with her troop, entire Samarkhand was alive along with her, and Taimur was seated on his throne with his head downcast, kerchief in his eyes, as if a bird has got wounded.

7

Istkhar was the domain of Armenian Christian. Muslims had conquered them, taken control of the area and slapped such regulations that Christians were living there in subordination at every step. The first ordinance was of Jijiya Tax, which every Christian was bound to pay, but Muslims were exempted from paying it. The second order was Church Bells would not be tolled. Third prohibition was about wines which Muslims used to consider ill-begotten. Christians actively opposed all these ordinances; and when the Muslim authority wanted to use armed forces for their observance, Christians revolted; they captivated the Muslim governor and hoisted the flag of Cross on the top of the fort.

Habib's was the second day today, yet how she was to solve the predicament?

Her pensive heart was of the opinion that these rules of bondage did not have any justification. All the religions should have been honoured equally; but Muslims would seldom be ready to lift these ordinances. And even if the Muslims of this area agreed upon it, why should have Taimur? True, there have been some broad-minded changes in his religious feelings, even then never would he be ready to okay lifting up of these regulations; in that condition does it bode her well to punish the Christians for their fight for freedom of religion? How could she kill that which she considered truth? No, whatever be the consequences, she had to keep up the truth. 'Ameen might think, that I am crossing my required limits, yet I won't bother? Next day by beatings of drums she announced: 'Jijiya is now hereby withdrawn. Bans on wines and Church Bells too are hereby lifted.'

These caused commotion among Muslims. They called it blasphemy, improper. Islam which Ameen Taimur had reared so carefully by the spring of his own blood, his minister Habib Pasha was digging at its roots. An order got topsy turvy. The army of the Sultanate got mingled up with local Muslims. Habib took shelter in the fort of Istkhar. Having gaind by the support of the armymen of the Sultan, the local Muslims became much more strengthened. They jointly lay a seize of the fort, and taking for granted that Habib has unleashed a rebellion, they sent a messenger to inform and apprise Taimur of the situation.

8

Half the night had been spent. For last two days Taimur did not have any information from Istkhar. Many types of premonition were cropping up in his mind. He was repenting as to why he allowed Habib go by his own, at all. Maybe, he is very sagacious; but in case the rebellion spread somewhere else, then with his handful of soldiers what he will be able to do? Certainly the rebellion might have gone stronger. The Christians there are extremely rebellious. Soon as they come to know that Taimur's sword has been rusted and he himself has developed liking for a life of palatial comforts, then their audacious courage would be doubled. In case Habib becomes surrounded by the enemies, then surely the hell would fall upon all.

Violently he slapped upon his thigh, changed his flank and then snubbed himself again. Why had he got so much demoralised? Have his brilliance and heroism left him already? One whose very name used to generate shudders among his enemies, is now ensconced inside his palace! In the eyes of the world this will only mean that no longer Taimur was a lion on the battle ground, but a lion engraved upon carpets. But Habib is an angel, who is not aware of the worldly vices; who is a god of mercy, simple-hearted, selfless; how should he know what a devil a human can turn out to become? During peace time his words can of course lead to community development and nation building. But his honeyed feelings do not have any sway in the battle ground, where devilish spirit storms the hour. In such hours, he only wins who can play colourful with human blood, or burn off grain-fields or barns, grows up forests by annihilating inhabitants. The rules of peace are at odds with the rules of battles.

Suddenly the watchman came in to announce the arrival of a messenger. The messenger kissed his hand and stood in official courtesy. He was so much engrossed in the instant awe of Taimur's imposing personality, that he forgot to tell what he had come to inform.

Beating his brows Taimur asked: What's the news? You came after three days that too at such hour in the night? The messenger kissed his hand kneeling down before him once again and said: Oh Khudaband! His Highness Wazir sahab has withdrawn the Jijiya Tax.

Taimur thundered: What do you say, withdrawn the Jijiya?

—Yes, Khudaband.

—Who did it?

—Wazir Sahab sir.

—By whose order?

—By his own order my lord.

—Hmnn.

—And huzoor, he also okayed for wine.

—Hmnn.

—Even the Church Bells have been okayed for tolling.

—Hmnn.

—And Oh, Khudaband, he united with the Christians and attacked the Muslims.

—Then what have I to do?

—Huzoor, you are our master. If you don't come out to help us, not a Mussalman would survive there.

—Ah, where's Habib Pasha at this moment?

—He is inside the Istkhar fort sir.

—And what Muslims are doing now?

—We have rounded up the Christians hidden inside.

—Also Habib, along with them?

—Yes, my lord, he has turned a rebel against you, my lord.

—And for this reason, my loyal servants of Islam have got him under seize. I believe, till I reach there, they would perhaps even kill him? You vile creature! Be off from my eyes. You Mussalman think Habib is my servant, and I'm his master! This is wrong, utter lies, the master of this Sultanate is Habib, Taimur is only his order-carrier servant. Taimur cannot question his decisions. It's undoubtedly right that Jijiya should be withdrawn. I don't have any earthly right to collect any recompense from people of other faith. No earthly right, understand? If *azaan* be heard from Masjid, why not bells to toll from the churches? There is no heresy in church bells' tolling? Do you hear, you the base man? There's no heresy in the sound of bell. Kafir is he who snatches away others due, who torments the have-nots, he who betrays or is self seeking. Kafir is not he who sees a streak of light in a place of clay or stone, who traces out Khuda's grandeur in rivers and hills, trees and bushes. He is more devout than us and you, who think Khuda is confined in masjid only. Perhaps you are thinking I'm uttering blasphemy. Mind you, it is blasphemy to consider other a Kafir. All of us are the servants of Khuda—all of us. Alright, now go back forthwith and tell those revolting Muslims, if they do not lift the seize immediately, Taimur would fall upon them like a devastating crisis.

The messenger stood dumb-founded as soon bugles were heard signalling some danger and forces began preparations for some battle-march.

9

On the third day as Taimur reached Istkhar, the seize of the fort was found withdrawn. But it was the canons of the garrison that welcomed Taimur. Habib thought Taimur had come to punish the Christians, whose hands and feet were all swollen with wounds, yet Habib was ready for the confrontation. She would not lament if her life be sacrificed for keeping up the Christians' dreams. No compromise could be reached at this point. If Taimur decided to reply at the shine of his sword he would be given a cunning counter-reply.

'But lo and behold! What the matter is this! The Sultanate army has hoisted the white flag? Taimur has come to make truce and not to fight. Welcome for him, therefore, has to be of different style.' Habib came out of the fort accompanied by the Christian leader. And to meet them it was Taimur all by himself riding fast towards them. Habib jumped out from her horse and bade adab.

In reply Taimur got down from his horse too and holding Habib's head lovingly planted a kiss on it and said: I have heard everything Habib. You did very well; and you did that which none else could have been able to do. I never had any choice to extort the Jijiya Tax or usurp the fundamental rights that the Christians have. Calling in a session of the assembly I will make it well ordained and thereafter I would launch some such good schemes which are coming to my mind for some times recently. And I hope you also would okay it. Well, any way you will have to.

The colour on Habib's face faded. Had her real identity been exposed to him? What kind of schemes did he mean? At Habib's heart came in turmoil.

With a smiling face Taimur asked: You were ready to fight against me?

Blushing Habib replied: Set against the Truth even Ameen Taimur would have lost his reality.

—Correct, doubtlessly! If you have heart of angels, you also have courage of lions. But my regret is what made you think, that Taimur would rescind what he had resolved? It's your victory over me, as you have made me understand that the Sultanate is not the estate of one fellow, instead it is such a tree every branch and leave of which are supposed to get the equal feed.

Both entered the fort. The sun had set out. Instantaneously a court was set in, and in the court Taimur accepted the pleas for rights to religious freedom for Christians.

From all corners came the happy prayers: Let Khuda increase the life of our Shahenshah.

Keeping up the tone Taimur said: My friends, I'm not the worthy recipient of your prayer. I'm returning you only what I had taken away by force. I'm not doing anything by which to acquire your good prayers. It is much more logical that you should curse me for keeping you deprived for so long of your rights.

Applause rent from all around: Maharwa, maharwa!

My dear friends, along with these rights of yours I also resign the Sultanate at your disposal. Because, all humans are equal in the eyes of Khuda, and no race or individual has right to reign over any other race. From today you are your own Badshah. I have hopes that at your level you also would not deprive the Muslims their rights. And if it so happens that any evil race try to snatch away your property from your hold, then Taimur would always remain disposed to your assistance.

10

Merry-making within the fort ended. The troop and the rulers have taken farewell. In the hall of the private audience, only Taimur and Habib were left. Upon Habib's face was streak of smile which greatly remained concealed under his seriousness. The reddish tinge on her cheeks was visible today. The headiness in her eyes, the fickleness in her limbs—none was seen ever before. Quite many times she behaved coquettish with Taimur, many times she laughed out with him, been merrily talkative exposing her youthful awareness, ignoring her position and rights.

Suddenly Taimur said: Habib, all your works I have kept uptil now. Today I should like to make a proposal of which I had spoken before, you know. You will have to agree with that.

With his palpitating heart Habib bowed her head and gracefully said: Kindly give me your command sir.

—First you promise that you'll accept it.

—I'm only your servant sir.

—No, you're my lord, light of my life, I would not be able to make out the bounteousness I have acquired from you. All long I have been holding this Sultanate as my most prized asset. I did everything for it, even the things which I should not have done. I stained my hands, with blood both of my own people and others. My work now is complete. I have made the base work complete, it's now your turn to build palaces on it. My entreaty is you become the Ameen of this Sultanate from today, during my life time, as well as when I am dead.

Habib's heart was flying high in the sky. She asked: Such a stupendous responsibility? Why? My shoulders are not such strong?

With a pitiable eagerness Taimur said: No, my dear friend, you'll have to make do with my entreaty.

In Habib's eyes there was happiness, but hesitation on her lips. Softly she said: Alright.

Overjoyed Taimur said: Let Khuda keep you secured well.

—But supposing you come to find out that Habib in reality is a virgin female of immature understanding, what happens then?

Then she would be the queen of my heart, at the same time when she is so to the Sultanate.

—Never you got bewildered?

—I know about it.

—Since when?

—When for the first time you had seen me with your cruel eyes.

—Well, how amazingly you concealed your revelation!

—You only taught me that. Perhaps none here knows about it, except me.

—How could you recognise me?

Taimur saw her with elated eyes and said: This I won't tell you.

It was this Habib, famed as 'Hamida', Taimur's begum.

❐

9. CONDEMNATION
(Dhikkar)

For Mani, orphaned and widowed, life now was rendered to nothing save lamentation. She was only five years old, when her father had died. Her mother somehow brought her up. At the age of sixteen she was pushed to marriage, by the help of neighbours; but within one year both her mother and the husband departed from this earth. In the predicament as was it Mani discovered nobody to give her shelter, but his own uncle Banshidhar. However the treatment from Banshidhar, she was meted out with ever since did not convince her that she could live there well in peace: though she was willing to withstand everything and do everything for them there. Abuses, snubbing, beatings all she would tolerate; at least nobody would cast aspersions upon her, besides, she would be protected from false stigma and from the reach of rogues and libertines. Banshidhar too was somewhat intrigued now by thoughts of upkeeping the family prestige. He could not ignore Mani's entreaty.

Yet after a few months Mani became convinced that her living with this family would not be possible for long. All the household chores she would do, would move to work at the slightest indication, would try to please everybody, even then for no reasons known to her both her uncle and the aunt used to feel resentful at her. Soon after her arrival the maid servant was removed. A lad was in the employ to help in bathing and washing, he too was removed. But despite Mani's salvaging so much of domestic works, both the uncle and the aunt used to fume at her.

Sometimes the aunt used to snub her, sometimes the uncle would to curse her, so much that even her cousin sister Lalita would hurl abuses at her every now and then. In the entire family only the cousin brother Gokul used to nurture sympathy for her. It was only in his talks some kinship, some affection were reflected. He was aware of his mother's nature. If he tried to make them appreciate the situation, or ever took side of Mani openly, her stay with the family would have been difficult even for a moment; hence his sympathy for Mani was confined only in giving her hopeful courage.

He used to tell: 'Sister, let me join a service somewhere first, only then your afflictions would come to an end. I would see then who dares to look askance at you. Your bad time lingers as long as I am yoked in studies.' These affectionate talks used to make Mani thrilled and with all her good senses she used to shower blessings onto Gokul.

2

That day was slated for Lalita's marriage ceremony. Guests were coming right from the morning. Tinkles of ornaments were being heard. At the sight of oncoming guests Mani too was being happy. Her face reflected happiness despite the fact that she did not have any ornaments to wear, nor was she given a beautiful saree to put on.

It was half the night worn out. The auspicious moment for the marriage was come. From the *janwasa* arrived the items for the bride's attire; the zeal to witness that she failed to forsake. She entered thc room with a smile on her face. Spotting her, suddenly the aunt shouted at her: Who has asked you to come here? Go away?

Mani had withstood much more insulting pains before that, but that day's snubbing pierced her heart as an arrow would. She began cursing herself. This is the reward of your frivolity.

What's your use in coming among the *suhagans?'* Dejected she came out of the room and began going upstairs to find out a lonely corner for shedding her secret tears. All of a sudden at the stairs she met with Indranath. He was Gokul's classmate and the bosom friend. He was an invitee too. He had gone upstairs in search of Gokul. Twice or once before he had seen Mani, and also had come to know that she was treated very indecently here. The lower echo of the aunt's talks had also reached his ears. Presently as he saw Mani moving upstairs he realised her mental condition and came upwards to console her; but the door was shut from inside. He peeped inside through the cracks in the door. Mani was shedding tears there, standing near the table.

Slowly he said: Mani open the door.

At this voice Mani promptly slipped into a corner, and asked modulating her tone grave: What do you want?

Indranath spoke appealingly: I'd fall on your feet in supplication, Mani, please open it.

Politeness soaked in affection as was that, was novel for Mani. In a world full of unkindness, could there be anybody who would speak to her in such beseeching overtone she never even had imagined in dreams. Her hand trembling in excitement, she opened the door. Indranath dashed into the room, and saw a coarse rope was hanging from the ceiling of the fan. His heart shivered in fear. Promptly he brought out a small knife from his pocket and said: What were you going to do, Mani? Do you know the punishment for this crime?

Mani replied bending her neck: Could there be any severer punishment than this? One, of whose countenance people feel aversion, if she be punished for her attempt to die, then I think there is no justice in the court of God.

Indranath's eyes became tearful. How harsh is the reality! Which was echoed in Mani's words! He replied: These days won't remain forever. If you think that you do not have anybody on this earth as yours, then it is your mistake. At least one man on this earth lives, to whom your life is more important than his.

Unexpectedly Gokul was seen coming. Mani went out of the room hurriedly. Indranath's words have raised storms in her mind. What was the meaning of his talks she failed to comprehend. Nevertheless, she began feeling as though her own life was come to a success that day. In her darkened life a glow of light seemed appearing.

3

Gokul had a misgiving as he saw Indranath seated there and Mani hurrying away out of the room. Natural composure of his face changed to give vent to harshness, as he said: When did you come here?

Unshaken, Indranath replied: I was here in search of you. As you were not found, I was about to go downstairs; but if I had left at that time, you might have found this room closed, and a dead body in it, hung from the hook of the ceiling fan.

Gokul mistook him forwarding excuses which he thought were his bid to conceal mischiefs. In pinching overtone he said: I did not expect of you that you would ever betray us by this.

Indranath's face reddened at the hint. He got up emotionally and said: Neither had I ever expected that you would hurl such a reproach at me. It was not known to me that you take me to be such mean and cunning. Mani could be an object of rebuke for you people here, but for me she would remain a person of respect. I do not feel the need to clarify myself before you, but for me Mani is much more pious a person than what might you be thinking her to be. I did not want that at this hour of celebration I would have the compulsion of speaking to you on this subject. For it (in fact) I was looking forward to find out a better opportune situation. Now that the point has come up, (I think) I have to speak today. I know only this much that Mani does not own any respect at your household here, but today having overheard your mother's talks, I have come to realise now, how low and renounceable you consider her to be. But for a trifle curiosity, driven by which she had gone to see joining others the items sent for the bride's dresses from the groom's party, your mother snubbed her off in a manner one would not do that even for a stray dog. You might well say here, 'what can I do there, what's my capacity to do anything at all!'

'It's shame for me even to drink water at a house such as it is where an orphan woman has to withstand so much torture. If you had made your mother concerned about it, during the initial days, things won't have come to this pass. But I cannot speak to your father and mother since you have the ceremony today at yours, however I don't have any hesitation to tell you that I would feel myself blessed to accept Mani as my life's partner. I had forethought to place this proposal after I have made some arrangement for me; but now, I am afraid, if I delay any further perhaps I will have to lose Mani forever; that is why, to relieve you and your people here, from any anxiety about Mani, I am placing this proposal.'

Never before in Gokul's heart welled-up waves of respect for Indranath as happened that day. He felt much ashamed as he had cast aspersion on him. At the same time he also realised that he was guilty of cowardice, as he remained indifferent to Mani's condition. This was only cowardice and nothing else. With an ashamed face he said: If mother has snubbed Mani on this, then it was her foolishness. I would ask her about it whenever I get the opportunity.

Indranath: Well, the time is over now for this asking business. I want, you should discuss this matter with Mani and tell me about it. I don't want she should stay here even for a moment. Only today I came to learn that she is a woman with strong self-esteem and if you ask me truly, I'd say, I am charmed at her nature. Such a woman, as is she, cannot stand torment.

Afraid, Gokul said: But do you know she is a widow?

When some unusual welfare is done by any of us we bring out all our defects unfolded in the open before that person. For, we become eager to show that we are not wholly deserving of such benevolence by the person.

Indranath smiled while saying: I know that. I have heard it, and that's exactly why I never could muster enough courage to ask your father. But, even if I did not know of it, that won't have affected my decision. Mani might be a widow, or untouchable or could even be baser than any, but to me she's a gem of women. For petty jobs we want experienced men; the person, with whom one of us have to spend our life, having experience in love we consider a defect. I am not one who would choke the voice of justice. Withstanding adversity is the best lesson of experience, nowhere was a school ever opened to teach how to acquire better experience of life. Well, one who has acquired a degree in such a school, we can certainly put in her hand the reins of someone else' life. Being a widow is not a defect in the woman, and for me it is her qualification.

Gokul was happy, said: I do not think my people at home are so much fools that they would object to it; but even if they do so in that case I prefer to keep my luck in my own hand secured. My elders have many rights upon an issue which I consider propitious for proper development of my soul, I would not like to be pressurised by anybody. I enjoy the pride that I am the builder of my own life.

Next moment Gokul expressed anxiety: And if Mani does not agree with the proposal.

Indranath took this fear absolutely baseless. He said: Now you're speaking childish Gokul. It's well accepted that Mani will not accept it easily. She would rather withstand kicks here in this household, tolerate snubs, abuses, yet she would like to stay here. It's not easy to wipe out age old superstition;

but we have to make her agree to it. The accumulated superstition in her mind have to be thrown out of her. I'm not very much in support of the remarriage of widows. I believe that the divine idealism in showing devotion to the dead husband in as invaluable jewel in this earth, and we have to do lot of fore-thinking before striking at this, if we must; but regarding Mani's case this logic does not apply. Love and devotion are formed not after names, but after humans. The man whom she did not even see for herself, with him she cannot be in love. It was only a point of rituals. We should not care for such pretentious show-off. Look, there, perhaps somebody's calling you. I'm also leaving now. In two-three days I would see you again; but see it doesn't happen that you keep on thinking and weighing upon it, while days pass out.

Gokul placed one of his arms around his neck and said: I would come to you, myself; the day after tomorrow.

4

The groom's party had left. Guests left too. It was nine in the night. Going to bed after marriage is the famous altogether, some on the pranks, some on floors, whoever got a place wherever was it, all were sleeping. Only Mani was arranging the rooms, and in the upstairs Gokul was reading a newspaper.

Suddenly Gokul called out for her: Mani, please bring a glass of water, for me.

Mani took a glass of water upstairs, kept that on the table, and turned about to return, when Gokul said: Wait a while Mani, I have something to speak to you.

Mani replied: No time now, brother; entire house is sleeping. If some pilferer sneaks inside not a utensil would be left spared.

Gokul said: Let him sneak in, had I been in your situation, I would have rather connived with the thieves to get all things stolen away. Look. I have to meet Indranath right now.

I have given him my word. Listen don't hesitate to answer me of what I ask you and answer quickly. If I'm late, he would be perplexed. Indranath loves you! Do you know that! Right?

Mani turned her face telling: You had called me only to tell this? I do not know anything.

Gokul: Anyway, that he knows and you too. He wants to marry you. Marriage will commence in *vaidik* rites. Do you okay that?

Mani's neck bowed down in shame. She could not tell anything.

Gokul said again: Father and ammi did not have the heart to tell you this; its reason you know very well. They might even cause you death by snubbing and inflicting constant torments, but never would they give consent for your marriage. If they do so they think that their name would be spoiled thereby. Its decision therefore is upto you. I think you should accept it. Indranath loves you, that apart, he is a spotless character and a courageous fellow of top order. Fear never touched him. I will get real delight if I see you happy.

In Mani's heart was surging waves of emotion, but she failed to utter a word.

Gokul spoke again, now insisting: Look Mani, it's not the time to remain silent. What are you thinking? Mani replied in pulsating voice: Yes. Heaviness upon Gokul's heart lighted. He began grinning. Blushed at that Mani ran out of the room.

5

In the evening Gokul said to his mother: Mother, at Indranath's place there is some festivity. His mother was alone worrying how all the works could be managed. I had said: I'll send Mani for help. If you permit, can I take Mani there. She will come back tomorrow or the day after.

At that time Mani came there. Gokul looked at her amusingly in the sly, Mani blushed at that. Nowhere could she find a way to go away from there.

Mother said: Why are you asking me? If she wants to go then take her.

Gokul said to Mani: Put on your dress and get ready. You will have to go to Indranath's house.

Mani objected: I am not feeling well, I won't go.

Gokul's mother said: Why don't you go? Is there a mountain to dig?

Mani put on a white saree and went out to sit at a tonga. Her heart was trembling in excitement again and again, her eyes becoming tearful. Her heart sank as though she was going to drown in a river.

As the tonga cleared some distance, she said to Gokul: Bhaiya, something is happening to my heart I don't know what! Better let us return home, I entreat you.

Gokul said: Are you mad! All the people there are awaiting you, and you are telling you are feeling nervous.

Mani: I am feeling some intuition that some ominous thing is going to happen.

Gokul: And my heart is telling you are going to become a queen.

Mani: Why don't you wait ten or five days? Okay, tell there, Mani is ill?

Gokul: Don't speak like a mad woman.

Mani: How heartily people would laugh at me!

Gokul: For an auspicious job I don't care about anybody's laughter.

Mani: Amma won't allow you to enter the house again. You too would face snubbings for me.

Gokul: I don't care. It's her habit only.

The tonga reached its destination. Indranath's mother was rational lady. She came out to receive the bride and escorted her inside.

6

As Gokul moved out from there towards his home, it was eleven o'clock. On one hand he had happiness over accomplishing an auspicious job, on the other hand he was afraid, what might he reply to people when Mani would not return home tomorrow. He decided, "Let me tell them clearly, when I reach home. It's useless to conceal. Why not today itself?"

Resolving this he entered home.

While opening the gate his mother asked: What had you been doing so late at night? Why did not you bring her along too? Who would do washing and cleaning of the utensils tomorrow in the morning?

Bending his head Gokul said: Perhaps she would never return amma. It has been so arranged that she will stay there permanently.

Mother stared in bewilderment asking: What are you babbling? Well, how could she stay there?

Gokul: She is married to Indranath.

The mother seemed to have fallen from heaven upon her head. Nothing could she control whichever came out of her mouth thereafter: You *kulangar*, tout, *haramzada*, and said many things one does not know what they meant. So much was it that Gokul's patience lost its limits. His face reddened, wrinkles on it set in as he replied: Amma, now stop it. I cannot stand to hear more than this. If I had done some unjust thing then I won't even raise my head even being beaten by your shoes; but I did not do any unjust thing. I did what was my duty under this circumstance, and which every other good fellow should have done. You are stupid. You are not aware how time is progressing. That's why patiently I listened to your abuses so long. It is painful for me to tell you, that both you and father had made Mani's life hell. You gave her afflictions which one won't give even to his enemies. Not because she was dependent on you, but because she was an orphan at yours. Now onwards she won't have to listen to your abuses. That day when the marriage ceremony was on, she was going to commit suicide, being wounded by some harsh words from none but you only. Had Indranath not gone upstairs that day, then all—we, you— all would have been in jail.

His mother replied with almost coquettish mockery: Ahaha! What a dutiful son you are, that you saved the entire family from a crisis. Why won't it be so? Now it was your sister's turn. Someday you take even me along and hang me upon somebody's neck. Then it will be all pleasure for you. This is the best style of earning. What would you do by studying?

Gokul writhed in agony; shocked, he said: Let not God make another boy be born off womb of a mother like you.

Having spoken this he moved out of the home and like a frenzied man he walked towards a direction. It was quite windy, yet it seemed to him that enough air was not there for breathing.

7

One week was spent; but no trace of Gokul was found. Indranath had got a job in Bombay. He had gone there. After arranging for accommodation he would send telegram then his mother and the wife would go there. Initially Banshidhar had a doubt that Gokul would possibly be hiding at Indranath's, but when he could not be found out there, entire township he began searching thereafter. All his acquainted people, friends, affectionate folks, relatives—but from all the places he received clear replies. Throughout day he would run and toil himself in searching him out, after he would return in the evening, he would rebuke his wife: Curse more your son. Shower curses upon him. I don't know ever you would gain any intelligence or not! If that witch-like girl has gone away, let her go, that means a burden has been removed from our heads. Keep a maid servant, your works would be done. When she did not come to live here, were we all suffering from hunger? Remarriage of widows are taking place all around, this is no unusual thing. Had it been within our control, we would have driven these supporters of widow marriages away from the country. We would have burnt them to ashes by hurling curses onto them, but these are not in our control. Apart from that, you did not even care to ask me. Whatever I would have considered good, I would have done, in that case. Or had you decided that I won't even return from office at all? And my last rites would be performed there itself? Only, you decided to fall upon the son with all your onslaughts! Now weep, with all your heart, opening that up.

It was dark already. Having scolded his wife Banshidhar was loitering around the door. Time and again his rage found a vent upon Mani, 'It's owing to this ogress that my house is ruined now. Who knows what was the ominous moment that she had come here, my entire family is raged to indignation. Had she not come why would I have to face such bad time to experience! What a brilliant was he! Who knows where has he gone?'

All of a sudden an old woman came to her and said: Babusahab, I have this letter for you, please take it.

With a leap Banshidhar went to the old woman to receive the letter. His chest was heaving with heart beats. 'Perhaps Gokul has written this letter.' But he could not make it out in the darkness. He asked: From where have you brought it?

The old woman replied: The gentleman who lives at Hussaingunj, now works in Bombay, it's his wife who sent it. Banshidhar went inside the room, switched on the lamp, and said: It is Mani's letter. She had written:- 'Respected chachaji, Please accept regards from this luckless girl. I am very much grieved to learn that Gokul has gone away somewhere, and till now he could not be traced out. I am the cause behind all this. Even this blot was destined to be imprinted on my face! That also is now done. You had to become so much grieved for the cause of me.

I am agonised at that; but I am confident Bhaiya must return soon. I am also departing for Bombay by nine o'clock train. Whatever sins I have committed kindly pardon me for all that, and also convey my pranam to chachi. I earnestly pray to God that Gokul Bhaiya return home all well. If God ordains, then at the time of Bhaiya's marriage I would be able to see your venerated feet and feel obliged.'

Banshidhar tore away the letter into pieces. He saw in the watch it was only eight o'clock. Forthwith he put on his dresses, came into the street, hired an *ekka* and left for the station.

8

Bombay Mail was placed at the platform. Passengers were busily moving all around. The loud calls from the vendors did not allow one to listen to anything. Time was almost come for the train's starting. Mani and her mother-in-law were seated in a ladies' compartment. In tearful eyes Mani was looking in front of her. Past, howsoever painful might that be, brings sweet memoirs. Mani was feeling happy recollecting those bad days. Who knows when again would she see Gokul! Had chachaji come here, she would have had his darshan. If he used to get angry with her at times, so what! That was for her benefit only! He would not come however. Now there is not much time left for the train to start. How could he come! The entire society would be agitated. 'God willing, when I come here again, then of course I would see him.'

All of a sudden she saw Lala Banshidhar coming. Promptly she came out of the compartment and stood there, then moved toward chachaji. She was about to fall upon his feet in supplication, but he moved backwards in indignation casting a threatening eye upon her, and said: Don't touch me, keep away, you luckless orphan. After throwing blots upon my face you also dare to write to me? Why did not you die? You ruined my family prestige. For you he left home, and still you are here giving me pains? Is there no water in the Ganges for you to die? Had I known about you to be so much unchaste and injurious, then I would have throttled your neck on the first day itself. Now you have come up to feign your devotion? Sinful woman like you should only die for good. The earth's burden will be lessened by that.

Hundreds of people had gathered around them in the platform and Banshidhar was showering abuses upon her. Nobody could make out what was the story, but all in their heart was condemning the Lala.

Mani was standing like a stone-idol, as though she was frozen there itself. All her feelings had been shattered. She was feeling, 'let the earth split open and I dash into it', or let some thunder fall upon her and her life—the base life as it is—come to its end. In presence of all these people she was thoroughly disgraced. Not a drop of tears came out from her eyes. In her heart was no tear. In place of that was a ferocious fire flaming inside, which as if was leaping upwards toward her head fast. Whose life on earth could be so much base?

Her mother-in-law called out: Bahu, come inside.

9

As the train started the mother said: Such a shameless fellow never have I seen. I got so much angry that I was feeling to pinch away his face.

Mani did not raise her head up.

Mother said again: Who knows, when those rotten people would acquire intelligence. He is even close to his last days. Why did not ask him, 'If your son has deserted you, what could we do about that?' Had he not been a sinner, why such a thunderlike misfortune would fall upon him?

Mani did not open her mouth still. Perhaps nothing was reaching her ears. Perhaps she did not have any awareness of her existence. With a fixed look she was gazing toward the window. Who knows what she was trying to find out from that darkness?

They arrived at Kanpur. Mother asked: Beti, would you like to eat something? Take some sweetmeats. Long it clocked even ten in the night.

Mani replied: I do not have the appetite now, amma. Later I would eat some.

Mother went asleep. Mani lay down too; but the countenance of Chacha was reflecting before her eyes and his words were ringing in her ears—'Ah! Am I so base, so much downgrade, that on my death the weight of the earth would lessen? What did he say? If you are a daughter of your parents, never again show your face. Yes! I won't show up my face! A face whereupon is so much blemishes, I don't have the wish to show up that again too!'

The train was running fast piercing the darkness. Mani opened her trunk, then putting off all her ornaments (from her body), put them inside the trunk. Then she brought out a photograph of Indranath, and for long she looked at it. In her eyes reflected a glow of pride. She kept the photograph inside and spoke to herself—'No, no, I can't blemish your life. You are God-like, you have done mercy on me. I was only atoning my early-rites. You only picked me up and took me in your heart; but I won't blot your life. You love me, you would tolerate for me all the dishonour and insult; but I won't be a burden to your life.'

The train was running fast piercing the darkness.

Mani kept on looking at the sky for so long hours when all the stars vanished and in the darkness she saw the reflection of her own mother—such bright, such realistic that she got startled at the sight and closed her eyes out of fear. Then again she saw inside the compartment, where another mother was sleeping.

10

How much of the night was spent who knows. Mother's sleep was broken at the sound of opening of the door; but her *bahu* was not there in the compartment. She rubbed her eyes, sat up and called: Bahu! Bahu! No reply came forth.

Her heart began throbbing. She saw at the upper birth, looked inside the privy, looked down under the birth, her bahu was nowhere to be seen. Then she went to stand at the open door. What happened to her bahu ! Who opened the door? No body came in the compartment, really? She began to feel very bad. She closed the door and began crying loudly, agonised. Whom should she ask? This was a mail train. Who knows, where would it stop next? 'I was telling her—Bahu, let us take seats at the gents' compartment. But she did not agree to it. She had said: Ammaji, you would not be able to sleep there well, Alas! This is the comfort she is giving me now?'

Suddenly she remembered about the danger chain. With all her strength she pulled the chain, again and again. Several minutes after the train came to a halt. The guard came. From the adjacent bogey a few more people came too. They all searched in the whole compartment. They looked into the lower plank. No trace of blood was there. They examined the furniture. Bedding, chest, box, the utensils, all were there. All were locked as well. Nothing was missing. Had anybody entered from outside, where would he had gone? It was impossible to jump away from the running train carrying a woman! Now, people after having analysed all these clues, came to the conclusion—supposing Mani had opened the door and wanted to look outside and suddenly her grips slipped away from the handles and she fell down consequently. The guard was a gentleman. He got down on the rails and upto one mile backward, both side of the rails, he tried to trace her out. No trace of Mani was there. What more could be done at night hours? Some passengers willingly shifted the mother to the gents' compartment. It was decided that the mother would drop at the next station and in the morning both sides be searched at far-off distance.

At the time of crisis we depend on others. The mother saw at one now, and at the other then. Her appealing eyes were perhaps entreating them all why somebody is not going to search out my daughter? Alas! the poor chap even had not her scarf of matrimony much used. With how much yearns and dreams was she going to her husband's. Why somebody was not going to that devil Banshidhar— 'See your heart's will is filled! Whatever you wanted has fulfilled! Even now your heart is not quenched!'

The old lady was bewailing seated in the compartment and the train was running fast piercing the darkness.

11

It was Sunday. In the evening Indranath was seated at the roof of his room accompanied by his two-three friends. They were exchanging jokes. Mani's arrival was the topic of their jokes.

One of his friends said: Why Indra, you have some idea about married life. What's your advise for us? Let us also make a nest, or should we so end our days sitting upon branches? From magazines only this much is apparent that between conjugal life and the hell there is a little difference.

Indranath replied with a smile: This is a game of fate, brother. Completely of fate. If in one condition married life is hellish, then on the other condition it is not less than heavenly.

The second friend said: Well, so much liberties cannot be there of course.

Indranath: Why so much? Even its one-hundredth won't be. If you want to return home at twelve in the night after daily shows of cinema, want to rise up at nine in the morning and having returned from your office at four, if you want to go to play cards, then you won't be happy in your marriage. And now that you get a suit stitched every month, after marriage you won't perhaps be able to stitch even one in a year.

Your shreematiji is coming today at night's train?

Yes, by the mail train, aren't you coming along with me to receive her?

Is it worth asking? Who's returning home now? But mind you, tomorrow you will have to give a treat.

Suddenly the telegraph department messenger came up to deliver an envelop containing the telegram to Indranath.

Indranath's face blossomed. Promptly he opened the telegram and read it. By reading once his heart had a sudden throb, his breath suspended, his head had a swirl. Eyes lost sight, as if the world was covered by a black veil. He threw the telegram towards his friends and covering his face by his palms began wailing bitterly.

Perplexed, both the friends picked up the telegram and reading it began staring at the wall dumbfounded. What had they been thinking, and what had happened.

One of the friends said: Some enemy might have despatched the false news?

The second said: Yes, sometimes some people play such mischiefs.

Indranath blankly looked at the telegram, did not tell anything.

For some time all the three men sat speechless stilled. All of a sudden Indranath stood up and said: I will have to avail this train.

The train left Bombay at nine o'clock in the night. Both the friends promptly packed his bedding and got him ready. One lifted the bedding and another the trunk. Indranath quickly dressed himself and went to the station. Despondence was ahead of him offering guidance; hope was following him bewailing.

One week had passed. Lala Banshidhar was seated at his door, when Indranath arrived there and offered *pranam.* Looking at him Banshidhar startled, not at his unexpected visit, but at his distorted plight; as though, the disaffected gloom was personified in his front, as if, the agonised 'ah!' has become manifest.

Banshidhar asked: You had gone to Bombay, no?

Indranath replied: Yes sir, today only I have returned.

Harshly Banshidhar asked: You even took away Gokul?

Indra replied setting his eyes at his ring: He is at my residence.

Why then he did not come here? Where did he meet you? Had he gone to Bombay?

No sir, yesterday as I alighted from the train, he was found in the station.

Then go and bring him! Whatever had passed was for good.

Having said this he rushed inside. Next moment Gokul's mother called him there indoors.

As he went indoors, the mother looked at him from head to feet.

Were you ill Bhaiya? Why is your health so much impaired?

Indranath did not answer anything.

Gokul's mother offered him a *lota* full of water: Wash yourself beta! Hope Gokul is alright? Where had he been all these days? Since then I sworn hundreds of pledges to gods. Why did not he come?

Indranath said, washing: I had told him to come to you. But he doesn't come here out of fear.

And where had he been all these days?

He tells, he was moving among villages.

Then have you returned from Bombay alone?

No, amma has come along with me too?

With a little hesitation Gokul's mother said: Is Mani hail and hearty there?

Indranath laughed: Yes madam, she is now living very happily. She's freed from all bonds of world.

Unbelieving the mother said: Go away you naughty boy! You are cursing the poor lass, but why did you return from Bombay so early?

With a wry smile Indranath replied: What should I have done else? Mother's wire I received in Bombay that Mani jumped from the running train to die. She was lying lifeless at Lalpur. I reached there rushing. Last rites I performed there itself. Today only we returned home. Now kindly pardon my guilt.

Nothing else could he speak. Rush of tears choked his voice. A letter he brought out from his pocket and placing it before the mother said: In her chest this letter was found.

For some minutes Gokul's mother kept on looking at the ground heart broken. Grief, and more than that the remorse had burdened her heart. Thereafter she lifted the letter to read.

'Swami,

When this letter will reach you I will bid adeu to this earth by that time. I am very much luckless, a woman. This earth does not have a place for me. You also would get only affliction and censure owing to me. I thought everything very well and have decided this, that for me it is only good to die. The kindness you had shown me, how can I repay that? In life never I wanted to get anything; but I grieve that I could not die keeping my head on your feet. My last entreaty to you is, you should not be agonised for me. May God keep you happy always.'

❒

10. THE COWARD
(Kayar)

The youngman's name was Keshab, and that of the young dame's Prema. Both were the students of the same college, in the same class. Keshab was a student of progressive ideas, antagonistic to barriers of caste and community. Prema was yielded to old mental impressions; thoroughly faithful to traditional glories and rituals; yet both were deeply in love and the talk had spread in the entire college. Keshab was a Brahmin, nevertheless wanted to fulfill his life by getting married to the vaishya-born Prema. He did not have concerns about his parents' disagreement to it. Even the argument on glory of birth (as Brahmin) sounded farcical to him. For him if there was any truth that was Prema, but for Prema moving even a step ahead without consent of her parents and of other members of the lineage was impossible.

It was evening. In one solitary corner of the Victoria Park, upon the sprawling green land, both were seated face to face. The strollers had left the place one by one, but the two were still there, hanging on. A talk was in the mid-way between them on such a topic that will not come to its natural solution by any means.

Keshab spoke annoyed: This means you don't have any care for me.

Prema replied trying to appease him: You are treating me improperly, Keshab. However, how can I raise this matter before my parents, it just doesn't come into my head. They are used in hackneyed ideas. Can you at all imagine the inhibitions which would crop up in their minds as they come to know of some such talks from my side?

Keshab asked rudely: So even you are slave to old beliefs?

Mild affection reflected into Prema's large eyes, when she said: No, I'm not slavish to these, yet my parents' wishes are more adorable to me than anything else.

— You don't have any personality of your own?

— Think something like this.

— I was under impression that such sham policies are meant for foolish women; but now I find even learned women like you also worship them. Now, since I am ready to forsake my whole world for you, I expect the same from your side too.

Prema thought: I don't have right on my own body. It was created in by those people, my parents, from their blood, who also brought it up with love and care; it doesn't own any right to act against their wishes.

Plaintively she asked Keshab: Cannot love be expressed as friendship, but only as wife and man?

Keshab retorted rudely: Look Prema, you'd rather make me lunatic, with your philosophising. I consider love as a tie of souls. Only be assured that I won't be able to live frustrated, I am a realist, and it is totally impossible for me to derive unrealistic pleasures from the world of fancy.

Having said so he took hold of a hand of Prema, and tried to drag her towards him. Prema jerked her hand off his clutch and said: No Keshab, I have told you, I am not liberated. You will not ask from me that in which I don't have any right.

Had Prema used harsh rebuke for Keshab, he would not have felt so much unhappy. For one moment he remained seated in dejection, then rose up telling in frustrated overtone: As you wish.

Slowly he dragged his feet away from there. Prema remained seated still shedding tears.

2

After the dinner as Prema lay down beside her mother, sleep would not drop upon her eyes. Keshab has said something which like a prolonged shadow in unsteady water lingered ringing her mind. Every moment its shape was changing. She was not able to make that steady. If she had to tell mother about it, how she would react? Diffidence would choke her voice. She thought, 'If I am married to Keshab, what else would remain left in my life, yet what can I do after all?' From this repeated thoughts one idea was settled in her mind, that she would not get married to anybody else save Keshab.

Her mother asked: Are you not getting sleep still? How many times had I told that you should do some domestic chores; but you do not have any time off your books. After a few days, you would have to own a different family, who knows what type of a family would be there in your life.

Ingenuously Prema asked: Why have I to own a different family, mother?

The mother smiled and said: This is the greatest distress of a girl, my child. She is brought up with love and care in the bosom of her parents, and soon as she grows up is given to belong to others. If she gets a good husband then all her life is spent in comforts, or she has to spend her days in tears. Everything is ordained, by luck. I don't find a family in our fraternity, wherein we can get your match. Nowhere girls are given due honour. Yet the match, we have to find out from the fraternity only. Nobody knows when this practice of ties over caste and community would come to break? Prema faltered while replying: Sometimes marriages take place out of the fraternity also.

She wanted to tell it so she did that, but the next moment her heart felt shivers lest her mother gets an inkling of her mind.

Surprised at her talk, the mother asked her: What! Did these happen among Hindu families somewhere?

Thereafter forthwith she herself gave answer to her question: Even if this has happened in a few families, how do they matter?

Prema did not reply this. She was afraid if mother would smell of her concern. Her future was like an open ditch, dungeoned, as if, it would swallow her up.

She did not know when she got her sleep.

3

Early in the morning when Prema woke up she felt a peculiar courage generated in herself. Sometimes we succeed in taking quite spontaneous decisions on all important issues: as if some divine powers drag us toward them; Prema's condition was the same. Until yesterday only she used to consider her parents' decisions honourable; but now having felt the crisis appear before her, she acquired the courage of that blowing wind in whose path came along some mountain. The very mild wind now would acquire tremendous power to climb atop the mountain and smashing its peak would blow out toward the yonder.

Prema was thoughtful in her mind: 'Suppose this body is given by my parents, yet whatever the soul within has to withstand is from this body itself. Hence considering anything upon this old argument was no longer unjust only, she considered that even suicidal. Why should she sacrifice her life after a false glory. She thought, if the basis of marriage is not love then that marriage is just a sale of body. Is it possible for one to offer herself without marriage? Her heart revolted at the very thought of her marrying off to an unknown youth.'

She was about to go to sit for her studies after the breakfast when her father called her in affectionately: I had been at your principal's yesterday. He was all praise for you.

Prema replied modestly: You only tell like this.

—No it is true.

While telling so he opened a drawer in his table, and brought out a picture framed in a velvet square; showing that to her he said: This boy has stood first in the ICS examinations. You must have heard his name?

Her old father had started such an introduction so that Prema would not understand his intentions, but she became anxious over the innate suggestion. Like an arrow her mind landed on the target point. Without looking at the picture she said: No I have not heard his name, of course.

Her father pretended surprise and said: What? You have not heard his name at all? In today's daily his name and life has been printed.

Prema replied drily: Maybe. But I don't attach any importance to the examinations. I believe those who take these exams are first class selfish. After all what else would be ambition of their lives, save that reigning over their own poor, the resourceless downtrodden brethren, and acquire enough wealth thereby. That is no high ambition in life.

In her refusal was fire, unfairness and cruelty. Father had thought Prema would be overjoyed at the description of the boy. But having heard her reply he said in sharp overtone: You are telling as though good family and powers have no importance for you.

Prema countered with a retort: Yes, I don't consider it worthwhile. I try to find out in man the attitude of sacrifice. I know such young fellows who would even give up these posts, even if these are imposed upon them by force.

Father said satirically: This is a new idea I have come across. On the contrary, I find people move around from one place to another for very petty jobs. I would like to see a boy for a while, who has such spirit of sacrifice. I would rather worship him.

Had that been a different occasion, Prema would have been downcast in shame, perhaps; but presently her condition was like the sepoy who had for his retreat only a yawning ditch, who had no other way out than to move ahead. She controlled her emotion, her eyes revolting, she went inside her room and sorted out, of many, one of Keshab's pictures, which in her look was the ugliest, and put that forward to her father. The old man wanted to ignore that but at the very first glance, he got attracted to it. His stature looked tall, and despite being weak it reflected a unity of constitution, health and restraint. His face was not bright with brilliance, yet had some such reflection of considerateness that generates in one's mind faith in him.

He saw the picture and asked: Whose is it?

Prema bowed her head in bashfulness, saying: He studies in my class.

—Does he belong to our fraternity?

Prema's face wore vague expression. Answer on this would decide her future. She repented in herself: 'Futile was it to bring out that photograph here to him.' The firmness that she had for a moment turned plaintive before this question. She replied in depressed tone: No sir, he is a Brahmin.

And with that promptly she came out of her father's room feeling hurt; as if, in the very air of the room she felt suffocated and standing behind the wall she began to weep silently.

At the first instance Lalaji became so much angry that he thought to call Prema back forthwith, and tell that it was impossible for him to okay this match. In the same huff he came after her upto the doorstep, but having spotted Prema crying there, his heart softened.

It was not concealed from him what Prema felt in her heart about the boy. He was a whole-hearted supporter of women's education; but at the same time he also wanted to keep up the prestige of his family. He was ready to spend everything for a groom from within her fraternity; however, outside that he was impatient to think of even the noblest born or the worthiest groom. He could not even imagine more vile an insult than this.

In rude overtone he said to her: From today you stop going to college. If education teaches you to wreck the family's prestige then that is bad-education.

Prema replied appealingly: But the exams are closeby!

Lalaji replied firmly: Let it be so.

He returned to his room thereafter and got to brooding.

4

Six months passed thereafter.

Lalaji came inside the household one day and called his wife in a solitary corner, then said: I have come to know so far that Keshab is a very gentle and talented boy. I am afraid Prema might even give her life off her pent-up grief over the issue. You tried to console her, I did, others did too; yet nothing had any effect upon her. Under the present circumstances what is the way out?

His wife replied worried: Alright, you would comply with her wish; but where would you live thereafter? O, how this evil girl was born off my womb, I don't know!

Lalaji frowned at this and scolded her: This I have heard a thousand times, now. But how long should we weep over our family prestige? If you have opened the cage of your bird and hoped that it will dance only at your courtyard, then you are mistaken. I have thought over the issue in cool brain; and have come to this conclusion that we should comply with such unavoidable distressful duty. On the pretext of family-prestige we can't kill Prema. If the world around laughs at us, let them do so, but mind you the days are not very far off when all these social prohibitions would come to break down. Even today hundreds of marriages have taken place having broken the bonds of castes and communities. If the purpose of marriage is to achieve a happy conjugal life, between a man and his wife, then we should no longer ignore Prema's claim.

The old lady felt harsh at this, then commented: If that's what you desire, why have you asked me then? Nevertheless, look here, I tell you, never would I come closer to her marriage ceremony, nor would I ever see her face in future. I'll console myself telling that she too has died for me, as have all my sons.

—Then what would you suggest me to do after all?

—Why don't you marry her off to that groom? What's wrong in that? In two years he would come successfully having cleared off his civil service tests. Comparatively, what does Keshab have against him? Maximum would he rise to become a clerk in an office.

—What if Prema kills herself? Then?

—Let her do so. You only give her incitement anyway. If she doesn't care for us, why should we blot our reputation for her? Killing oneself is no easy job. It's only a threatening. A wayward horse, remember, would not allow anybody lay his hands on it until is yoked in harness. Besides, when her mind is of such fickle type, who can say, she would spend all her life with Keshab alone? As she is in love with him today, tomorrow she might be so with somebody else? Otherwise, what's your intention, do you want to cause yourself excessive insult and harassment in the fraternity?

Lalaji looked at his wife in questioning eyes and said: What if she goes to Keshab tomorrow all by herself? And gets married? What would you be able to do then? There again how much of your prestige will be left to boast of? Maybe, owing to her shyness, or for the respect she has for us, she still is staying home, but if she resolves to do otherwise out of obstinacy, you and I would not be able to stop her from doing anything.

The problem, as was this, could have such terrible consequence, the old lady never had even imagined. The question was like a fire-ball that landed on her head.

For a moment she kept seated dumb-founded, as if the assault had smashed her conscience. Defeated thereafter she replied: You think of the unthinkable fancies. Never had I heard from anywhere that a noble-born girl got married by her own moves.

—You might not have heard; but I have heard; and I have seen, and it is quite possible to happen so.

—The day this would happen, you won't find me alive.

—I don't say that this would happen; but it is so possible.

—If this is likely to happen, then it is better that we should arrange to do something. If the nose is to cut off, then why not chop it off with a sharper blade. Call Keshab tomorrow rather, see what he has to tell.

5

Keshab's father was a government pensioner, peevish and miserly. He used to get peace only in the show-off religion. He was short of imagination. He never could honour other's wishes. Even today he belonged to the same old world, wherein he had spent his childhood and youth. The surging animation of the new age, he used to call calamity and wanted to save his own family from its onslaught, at least all by his two hands and two feet; that is why, as Prema's father went to him one day and proposed Prema's match with Keshab, the old Panditji failed to keep up his self-control. Staring at him with his blurred vision he countered: You have not taken *bhang,* I hope? Such a match, whatever be it, is not marriage. I have a feeling you too have caught the airs of the new generation.

The old Babuji (Lalaji) said politely: Such a match I myself would not like to approve of. On this issue my views are the same which are yours; but things have come to such a pass that helplessly I have had to come to your counsel and service. You know very well how self-willed have become the boys and girls of these days. For us, the old people, it has been difficult to uphold our ideas. I fear, if they are frustrated they might play terribly with their own lives.

The old Panditji stomped his feet upon the ground and roared: What do you say, sir? Don't you feel ashamed? I am a Brahmin, and even among the Brahmins, I am noble-born. Howsoever downgraded they might have gone, they are still not so much inglorious, that they would move around marrying girls from bania-bakkal families. The day girls from noble-born Brahmin families would be scarce, such a problem might arise then. But I ask you, how could you dare to raise this matter before me?

More the old Babuji was submitting himself, more angry the Panditji was getting. At last Lalaji could not stand his insult any longer and cursing his own fate he left.

At that time Keshab returned from the college. Panditji promptly called him and asked rudely: I have heard, you have already tied yourself in marriage with a daughter of a trader. How far it is true?

Keshab feigned ignorance, said: Who told you that?

—Somebody told me so. I'm asking you, is it true or false? If it is true, and if you have resolved to blot the prestige of your family, then for you there is no place in this house. You would not get even a dime of my savings. I am within my rights that I would give that to him whomever I would like. Having done this impropriety, you cannot step in my house.

Keshab was well aware of his father's nature. With Prema he was in love. He wanted to get married to Prema secretively. His father won't live long. In his mother's affection he had faith. In the waves of love he was ready to withstand all the distress, it appeared; yet like a coward sepoy who loses heart in front of a gun and moves back steps, became the plight of Keshab. Alike common youth he could talk and debate high over ideals; verbally he could swear before them for his own devotion to the ideals; but he did not have the courage to stand afflictions for these ideals. If he stuck to his insistence and his father to his resolve, then what might happen to him? His life itself would be spoiled. He said in a suppressed voice:—Whoever is telling you this, is telling absolute lies.

Panditji asked staring at him hardly: So, this information is all false?

—Yes sir, absolutely false.

—Then today only you write about it to that Bania and then mind you, if such talks ever arise again, then I would be your worst enemy. Now, go away.

Nothing else Keshab could speak out. From there he moved away, it appeared his feet had no strength.

Next day Prema wrote to Keshab a letter: 'Dear Keshab,

Having heard the account of ill-mannered and insulting treatment that your venerated father has given to Lalaji, many, doubts are surging in my heart. Perhaps he has scolded and abused you too. In such a state of mind, restlessly I am eager to know your decision. With you I am willing to withstand all kinds of difficulties of our life. I am not attracted to your father's property, I only want your love and be happy in that. Today in the evening please come to ours for dinner. Both my father and mother are eager to see you. Presently, I am immersed in the dream, of that moment when both of us will be tied in a bondage which does not know how to break, which would remain united even in mighty danger.

I am yours only, Prema.

Evening fell, yet the answer to her letter did not come. Her mother asked time and again: Keshab did not come as yet?

Old Lala was seated also looking out to the door for him. Even it came to be nine o'clock, neither Keshab came in, nor his letter.

In Prema's heart were upheavals of different thoughts and alternatives, repeatedly; perhaps he did not get scope to write the reply, or maybe he did not get time to come today, tomorrow must he come. She read once again all the love letters Keshab had written to her before. From each word of the letters abundant love dripped. What vibes in them, how restless, what soulful yearn! Soon she recollected Keshab's words, which he had told her hundred times. How many times he had wept before her; yet even after all these for the entire night her mind, it seemed was suspended upon an impale.

Early in the morning Keshab's letter came. With her hand trembling, Prema received the letter and read it.

Soon afterwards it dropped from her hand. It appeared that her life-blood has clotted. It was written:

'I am in great predicament as to what I should write to you. Here, upon this issue I have thought in cool mind and have arrived at such conclusion that under the present circumstances it is intolerable for me to ignore my father's instruction. Don't consider me a coward. I am not selfish either; but the obstacles I have before me here, I do not have the power to conquer over them. Better you forget our old talks. I had no thought of these obstacles at that time.'

Prema took a long, deep, burning breath and torn away that letter. Tears flowed down from her eyes. The very Keshab whom she had accepted in the core of her heart with love and submission, could become so much cruel she never had the least expectation. It seemed, like she was amid some golden dream ever since, which vanished soon after as she opened her eyes. If hope was gone from life, then what she was left with save the dungeon ? She, as if, had loaded a boat with all the treasures of her heart and soul, that boat was drowned in waters. How could she manage to load another boat? If that boat has been drowned, she too would drown herself with it.

Mother asked: Is it Keshab's letter?

Her eyes downcast, Prema replied: Yes, his health is not well.

What else she could have said save this much? She did not have the courage to face shame by telling about Keshab's cruelty and hollow-heartedness.

The whole day she remained yoked in domestic works, as it were, she was absolutely free from any worry. At night she served meals to all, ate herself as well, and upto the late hours of night sang playing her harmonium.

But when the day broke, her lifeless body was found in her room. In the golden rays of the morning sun was reflecting the glow of life from her yellowish face.

❐

11. HUNTING
(Shikar)

Clothed in tatters Munia looked at the moonlike beautiful face of Rani Basudha in reverence and lifted the young Prince in her lap. While saying: 'How, we the poor can pull on like this, Maharani! For me, I would not even spend one single day with my man! I would not have even allowed him sit at my house! Such filthy abuses would I have hurled upon him that he would have been forced to be in tight corner.'

Rani Basudha tried to tease her with mock seriousness: 'Why? Won't he ask you, 'Who you are to meddle into my affairs! Whatever I would feel like I would do? You should only concentrate in realising your fooding and clothing. What have you to do with my other things? I'm not your slave.'

It was only three days since Munia was employed a maid to play with the little son. Earlier, she had worked at two or four families for cleaning of utensils; however she never could adopt herself to speak to the queens in appropriate manners. The dark complexioned and withered physique of hers became agitated. In rude overtone she said: The day he would utter such talks, I would uproot his moustaches. *Sarkar,* as he is not my bonded-man so am I not his bonded-maid? Again, if he becomes my slave, then I am of course his bonded-maid. I do not eat myself, but feed him always because he is a male fellow. He requires to do great toil and pain in portage. I myself would choose to wear tattered clothes, but never I allow him do that. If I can do so much for him, then can he have the cheek of casting a threatening eye at me?

A man covers his roof so that in rains or drizzles he can be sheltered. Who would like to live in a house, who has the fear as to when the house might collapse. Better than that is the shade under the frontal part of the house. Yesterday, I don't know where he was busy, in music and fun. He returned home by ten at night. The whole night I did not speak to him. When he fell upon my feet for pardon, appealed constantly, only then I felt pity on him. That's the only drawback I have. I cannot stand to see dejection in his face. That's why at times he goes astray but now I am quite firm. If once he quarrels with me again, either he stays at home or I do. Why should I tolerate somebody's coercion, *sarkar*. One who lives on his earning, should do so. I earn equal to his.

Basudha asked again in serious mood: Had he had maintained you by keeping you within home, would you have withstood his blusters?

Munia seemed out to fight. She replied: Who can maintain anybody, *sarkar?* When my man works outside, I also work inside. Why? Nothing is spent in doing domestic chores? From outside works one gets relief in the evening. But from domestic works one doesn't even get relief even at night. If my man wants, he would move around and entertain himself, keeping me away in the domesticities, well that I won't be able to tolerate. While telling this Munia went out with the Prince on her lap.

Basudha glanced beyond the window of the room with tired woolly eyes. Outside was a sprawling green garden, flowers of many colours in which were to be seen from within clearly, and on its background, an enormous temple with its golden head plunged high into the sky, was looking eye to eye with the sun. Decorated in many- coloured dresses and ornaments women were coming in to worship the deity. On the right side of the temple was a pond in which lotuses were all in smiles, and amid the cool of the *Kartika* the sunrays were spilling forth the glowing liveliness. All this soothing beauty of nature, however, could not give Basudha happiness. She rather thought, nature was casting satiric smile on her plight.

On the bank of the pond stood a dilapidated hut of a boatman, as though, it was in tears like a hapless old woman. Basudha's eyes became filled in actual tears. Standing amid flowers and the garden, that empty hut offered a lively picture of its soul, despite surrounded by luxury and abundance. She felt like, 'let me go to the hut, embrace it with all my heart, and weep over it non-stop.'

It was five years since Basudha came to this family. Earlier she lived upon her luck. The youngest of her parents she left her joyless hut to live into a large building; where wealth seemed to kiss her feet. At that time wealth was everything to her. Love to her husband was a secondary choice; but gradually her greedy mind could not remain happy only with wealth; she began to reach for her husband's love. Within a few days she realised, 'I have also acquired the gem of love'; but by and by this illusion began fading away. Kunwar Gajraj Singh was handsome, broad-minded and strong, educated, fun-loving and knew well how to do acting of love; however, in his life there was no wire that would vibrate with real love. Basudha's blooming youth and colourful beauty, which might even lure gods, were to him mere objects of fun-making. Suppressed under sensational merry-making like horse-race, hunting, *satta* and *makar,* the love had turned to become pale, insipid; having been deprived from true love thereby, Basudha's yearn had only to castigate her own fate.

She was not happy even after getting two gems of sons. Kunwar Sahab had since gone to hunting, for more than one month and was yet to return. And that was not the first similar happening. Yes, this time his schedule was extended. Initially, he used to return by one week, thereafter two weeks became common, and at times he used to be traceable only after one month schedule. About three-four months in a year he began fixing for his preys. After he was back from hunting the tune was set for horse-races. Sometimes Meerut, sometimes Puna, sometimes Bombay or at times Calcutta. If at times he used to stay at home, the hours would be spent in brags and boastings with his rich companions, the sons of noblemen. At such hues and demeanour of her husband, Basudha used to fret out herself and was melting away. Of late, she also developed mild fever.

For quite long Basudha sat there watching the picturesque sight. Thereafter she walked to the telephone and asked the manager of the estate: Is there any letter from Kunwar sahab?

The reply came through the phone : Yes madam, just now a letter is received. Kunwar sahab has killed a very big lion.

Basudha flared up as she asked: I am not asking this! What has he written about his return?

—Well, there is nothing written about his return, madam.

—How far is his camp from here?

—From here! Not less than two hundred miles. Hunting is going on at the jungles of Pilibhit.

—Please arrange for two motor-cars for me. I want to go there today.

Reply came through the phone after a few minutes: One motor-car he has taken away with him. Another is sent to the district magistrate's bungalow. The third is on service of the bank manager. The fourth is being repaired.

Basudha's face fumed up in anger. She asked: By whose order motor-cars have been sent to the services of bank- manager and district magistrate. You call both the cars back. I must go tomorrow.

—Always motor-cars are sent to those two sahab. So I have sent them today also. Now since you have given instructions to call them back, I will do it.

Having finished the calling Basudha moved about to arrange for her journey. With the same vein she decided to settle her luck.

Not like a forsaken wife would she end up her life. She would go and tell Kunwar sahab, 'If you think that I would like to live as a maid among your other property, then that's not to be tolerated by me. May your property be auspicious to you! I have to claim my right upon you, and not on your property. If you want to distance yourself a grain-length from me, then, I will distance myself a hand-length from you.' So much of chagrined talks were heaving up in her mind like whirlwind.

Doctor sahab called from the door: May I come in?

Basudha replied politely : Pardon me today. I am going to Pilibhit a while from now.

Worried Doctor said: You are going to Pilibhit? But the temperature you have will rise! At the present state of your health I can't advise you go to Pilibhit.

Annoyed Basudha replied: If it rises, let it happen so. I'm not worried about it.

Old Doctor waved aside the curtain of the door, came inside the room and looking at Basudha's face said: Come on, let me check your temperature. If your temperature is risen, then I'm not allowing you to go by any means.

—No need to checking my temperature, my decision is final.

—To be careful about your health should be your first duty.

Basudha replied with a smile : You can rest assured. I'm not going to die early. Besides if the medicines of any disease is death, then what after all you would do?

For once or thrice the doctor insisted, then amazed at the pass, he nodded and returned.

2

If one were to come by train, after the terminal station he had to cross ten kos-long lonely stretch of road within jungles which is why Kanwar sahab always used to cover this road by motor-car. Basudha also decided to come through that route.

By then both the cars arrived. Basudha gave vent to her anger upon the drivers telling, 'From onwards if you ever take the motor-car anywhere without my permission, mind you, I will cut from your wages the whole money earned from the renting of the cars. What a joke! In-house people would suffer, and others would enjoy? These motor-cars are maintained for our comforts, not for others' flattery. If anybody has fancy to ride motor-car, he should buy it for his own and not should he try to impress in frustration. He should not sit down to show-off by reading from Koran as soon he finds a sweetmeat shop.

As she moved to start both her children stirred up to accompany, but when they were pacified with the talk that their mother was going to far-off places to kill the bugbear, they instantly drew cold feet about going along with their mother. Since morning that day Basudha never did caress them with a burning envy she had conjectured, 'Why me alone to caress them, well have I to take their stake all by me alone? He would enjoy himself and feel comfortable outside, and I alone have to be seated with them holding them tight onto my bosom? Yet at the time of departure her motherly heart yearned for them. Both of them she held tight to her lap caressing by turn, hugged both and after assuring them of her return within an hour, she moved out of the palace in tearful eyes. Also, time and again memory of her children came to her mind, during her journey. Many villages came to her route, little boys were coming out of their houses, to witness the car race and were clapping after them standing on the roadside mimicking the car-drives in fond likes. Basudha was feeling so much to lift them onto her lap, and hug them for a while. Faster the cars were speeding ahead, faster were fleeting her mind along with the passing trees in her view. Several times she felt, 'Let me return home. As he doesn't have a bit of concern about me, why should I risk my life over my cares for him? If he likes he might come along, if he doesn't, but she could not ignore temptation of taking on him right and left once having met with him. Her body was aching from dead tiredness, she also was having fever, her head as though was splitting from pain; yet she suppressed all these obstacles from her ailment by help of her unflinching determination and was going ahead. So much was it that, as she reached the dakbungalow in that corner of the jungles at ten o'clock in the night, she was unconscious of her physical condition with high temperature racking herself.

3

Hearing the chauffeur's call Kunwar sahab came out and asked: How come you? Here at this spot? Everything is alright at home!

The chauffeur came closer and replied: Rani saheba has come, *huzoor*. She has developed fever at the journey. She's inside the car unconscious.

Kunwar sahab stood there surprised and asked in harsh voice: Why then did not you take her back? Don't you know that any hakim-vaidya can't be traced out here!

The chauffeur felt himself in a fix, replying: *Huzoor*. Never did she agree with the idea, by no means. What else could I have done?

Kunwar sahab rebuked him: You shut up! Do make only stories! You had thought out a plea to witness the funs of hunting and sleep lying unconcerned after that. You never perhaps asked her go back at all!

The chauffeur: She was snubbing me for that, *huzoor*!

—Had you said that to her?

—I did not tell her that, of course!

—Then stop it. I know you very well. Look, right away you will have to return by motor. Who else is there along with you?

In a depressed tone the chauffeur said: There's beddings and garments in one car. Rani saheba is seated inside the other one.

—That means no body is there along with her!

—*Huzoor*, I am only an order-carrier.

—Oh, shut up!

Kunwar sahab fumed in anger; then went to Basudha with a care-torn heart and softly called her. There came no reply from her, tenderly he placed his hand on her head. Her head was like a hot plate; the same heat, as it were, had sucked all her anger and pent-up grievances. He left back to the bungalow, awakened up all the sleeping people, spread the bedding and thereafter lifting up Basudha tenderly to his lap he lay her down on the bed. Then taking position near her pillow, in painful eyes he looked upon Basudha. Upon her dirt-smeared face and disorganised dust-layered tufts of hairs today he saw flashes of yearning for love. Since long had he observed Basudha a luxury- loving person, who never really cared for his love. Who was busy in her make-up and adornment only. Today he was gazing at her womanhood, made-up in powder and pomade of dust. How great was her eagerness, how much was the erotic feelings, plunged into the pleasure of her sortie, now at the door of exit of the cage she was fluttering her wings. Would he not welcome her by opening the cage-door?

The cook asked: Well, has her majesty come unescorted?

Tenderly Kunwar sahab replied: Oh yes, what else! So many people were there in the palace, she did not take any of the escorts. Comfortably could she come by train. From this end, we could have sent the motor-car to the station. It's only her feelings. And what high temperature she has got, I can't even keep my hand on her forehead. Now, here, warm up some water, and cook some food for her.

The cook flattered uttering in his master's voice: Hundred *kos* make a great distance, my lord. Whole day she spent just keeping seated.

Kunwar sahab straightened the pillow under Basudha's head and said: Even we are rendered unmoveable at such a journey.

We cannot even be able to straighten our waist for two days, what to talk of her majesty's! Nowhere in this world might there be a nonsensical road as this one.

While speaking this he brought a small bottle of oil, and began massaging some of that upon Basudha's forehead.

4

Basudha's fever did not remit until it was twenty first day. The doctor of the family was called in. Both the boys, Munia, servants, employees of the palace—all were called in. Paradise was created in the wilderness.

Lying on her bed Basudha remained under constant nursing of Kunwar sahab and derived ecstasy and contentment thereby. He was in the habit of sleeping till the day wears on, but now much early he would get up, work with all his heart and soul for her food, and care meticulously for every detail of her comfort. For a few minutes only he would take leave for his bath and lunch, and then immediately he would return to sit beside her bedside. He was spending his days as though doing penance. His health began to deteriorate, his countenance began lacking lustre of health. He would remain much depressed.

One day Basudha said: Why don't you go to hunting these days? I have come to accompany you in hunting. God knows what ominous hour was it when I started, that I ended up in making you do penance for me. Now I'm alright; but please look at yourself in the mirror.

For all these days Kunwar sahab did not even have a mind to go for hunting. Talks on this subject was also not frequent. Coming and going of hunters, mixing up among themselves were all stopped. An accompanying hunter once has raised the talk of hunting down of a lion, Kunwar sahab looked at him in such rude eyes that he seemed vaporising out. He derived pleasures in sitting beside Basudha, in speaking to her to amuse her, in preparing medicine and food for her. All his luxury and enjoyment seemed wiped out of his life amid the harsh penance. He was found quite often drawing imaginary lines upon Basudha's palms with much attention. From any corner if ever he overheard even a talk of hunting he looked at that direction in fiery eyes. As he heard the same talks from Basudha he became unhappy. She still considered him addicted to hunting. In melancholic overtone he replied: Yes, what else should be the better time for going out to hunting!

Basudha insisted: I am alright, true! Look (indicating toward the reflection of the mirror) there is no paleness in my face. But you of course are going to be sick. By going out you will feel better. Sitting beside illness one becomes ill.

Basudha had said a simple talk; but in the heart of Kunwar sahab that inflicted a sparkling. Several times of late, he had been repenting of his craze for hunting. Had he not been after hunting so ardently, then Basudha would not have come, nor would she have fallen ill. He was very much dejected at this. To her he did not reply anything at that time. Perhaps nothing could he speak, he continued to draw imaginative lines upon Basudha's palms.

In the same simple vein Basudha said: Which are the gifts you have acquired this time? Ask them to bring here, let me have a look at them. I'll take the best of them for my collection. And now onwards also will go along with you for hunting. Tell me, would you like to take me along? I am not going to budge away from it. Don't give me excuses.

Showing off his hunted gift was a mania Kunwar sahab had. Hundreds of hides he had collected. Many of his carpets, couches, cushions, chairs, wicker stools were made of hides. Even the wrappers and beds were made of hides. He had many of his suits tailored of hides of tigers. During hunting he used to put on those suits only. That time also he had collected many horns, hides of heads, paws of animals. Surely Basudha would be entertained by those things. But this he could not realise that having failed to enter through the main gate, Basudha had endeavoured to come through the back doors. Promptly he went to gather those things by help of his people; but kept them awaiting behind the curtain and instead, he himself returned to Basudha; afraid 'lest Basudha does take ill of my eagerness'.

Eagerly Basudha asked: Have you brought the things?

—Yes, I have brought them; what if the doctor sahab comes here suddenly?

—Doctor sahab has only advised to refrain from reading and writing.

The gifts were brought in. One by one Kunwar sahab unfurled them out before her. Glow of happiness reflected in Basudha's face which was not seen for weeks; as if some boy had gone forgetful at a show. After illness often we become childlike—as much adamant as distressed and artless. The books in which we never had interest are read after illness. Basudha seemed dancing in the lap or revelry. There were hides of leopards, tigers, deer, boars, etc. With a new zeal Basudha examined them like examining pictures of biscope coming one after another. Each of the gifts had a history, Kunwar sahab narrated all. How this animal was killed? Which were the troubles that appeared before its death? How many trickeries were to be adopted before actually killing it? Where exactly the first shot had hit it? All. Basudha listened to each story with astonished eyes. Such liveliness, thrilling agility and entertainment never she had in any poem, song or merry-making. The most beautiful of all was hide of a lion. That she chose for herself.

That was, however, Kunwar sahab's costliest of the items. He had decided to hang that in his own room. He said: You better pick up one from hides of a tiger. Because this one is not as good.

Basudha dragged the hide toward herself and said: Oh, leave aside your suggestion. I would take the bad one only.

As though he was wiping off his tears, Kunwar sahab said: Okay, you take that. I was only telling considering your wish to keep the best. Another typical I would hunt down again.

—Then why were you dodging me?

—Why after all would I dodge you?

—Alright, then swear upon my head, it is not the most beautiful skin.

Kunwar sahab smiled conceding defeat: Why to swear upon you? Just for the hide? Even if I have lakhs of hides such as this, I would love to present all of them to you.

After the hunter took away all the hides, Kunwar sahab said: Upon this hide I will write my dedication in black wool.

Out of fatigue Basudha stretched along the bed, telling: From now onwards I also would go along with you to hunting.

Soon thereafter she began to imagine, she too would kill a lion, and its hides she would gift away to her husband. Upon it she would write in black wool: 'My Dearest!'

The light which had dimmed pushing many actions and many items under gloomy covers, now began to be brightened again.

5

Basudha developed irresistible proclivity in hearing the details of hunting games. Many times Kunwar sahab had to narrate his experiences. However she was never satiated from it. Since long Kunwar sahab's world was different, about sorrows and pleasures wherein, or of its losses and gains, its hopes and disappointments Basudha had no concern. In the whole business of this world Basudha had no taste, rather she had the distaste, in it. Kunwar sahab too used to conceal from her all the affairs of this world, so different to her, but now Basudha turned out to become a bright light of the games, rather like a goddess blessing boons upon this world.

One day Basudha insisted: Teach me how to shoot from a gun.

Securing the doctor sahab's permission was not delayed, hence. Basudha had fully recovered. At an auspicious hour Kunwar sahab initiated her into it. From that day always was she found practising aims at the targets under shadow of a tree, and standing closeby used to be Kunwar sahab, taking her tests.

The day she shot down her first bird, Kunwar sahab's joy knew no bound. Servants were paid tips; Brahmins were given gifts. To memorise the auspicious happiness the lifeless bird was procured as a mummy.

In Basudha's life now ushered in a new inspiration, a new kind of thrill, a novel hope. Her deprived heart was not scared out of evil imagination like before. Now she had faith, strength and love.

6

After several days Basudha's ambition came to be fulfilled. Kunwar sahab agreed to go to hunting taking her along, and the prey was a lion. That too one which had created havoc among people of the nearby villages.

All around was dark, such dungeon that the earth seemed panting under its weight. Kunwar sahab and Basudha were ensconced controlling their respiration at a high raised platform (in the deep jungle) wielding their guns. That was a terrible animal. Only last night it has dragged a sleeping man away from the platform raised high in his field. At its cleverness people bit fingers in fear. His platform was so high that even a leopard was not able to leap onto it. Yes, it had noticed that the man was sleeping on the platform, keeping his head toward the barriers. The evil animal applied a trick. It went to a nearby village and from there picked up a bamboo. One side of it it chewed to crush, and when enough broom was made out of it, it held the other end of the bamboo tight may be by its front paws or by its mouth and brushed the man's head with the broom. It was aware of the fact that his hairs would get fastened into the brooms, which actually happened. Then on one big jerk the hapless man was dragged onto the ground. To strike down that man-eater devil, the two hunters were cautiously in wait. Down afar a buffalo was fastened to a stake and the lion's arrival was looked forward to. Kunwar sahab was still; but Basudha's heart was throbbing out of excitement. With the slightest shaking of leaves she was getting startled, and instead of aiming her gun toward that direction, she was frightened enough to cling together with Kunwar sahab. Hence Kunwar sahab used to encourage her time to time.

—Soon as it would fall upon the buffalo, 1 will clear it away from this world, turn of your shooting at it would not come at all.

Basudha shivered at the thought: And what if it springs up in case the aim is missed.

—Then second shot will be fired. Three guns are loaded ready. You are not terrified, no?

—Not at all. 1 want rather the first shot will be from me.

Leaves murmured. Basudha startled and coiled around her husband's shoulder. Kunwar sahab put his hand upon her neck and consoled her: Take your heart, darling. Basudha became ashamed: No, no, I am not afraid. I got a bit startled.

Suddenly, two fire balls were seen brightening near the buffalo. Kunwar sahab softly pressed Basudha's hand and made her aware of the lion's appearance. Himself he became live-wire. As the lion fell upon the buffalo he fired at the target. It missed. Second fire he shot promptly, the animal was wounded, but did not fall. Maddened by anger it roared so loud that Basudha's heart got panicky with consternation. As Kunwar sahab was about to fire third time, the lion lept toward the platform. At the bang of its frontal paws, the platform was shaken so fiercely that Kunwar sahab fell down from it at the impact, with his gun at his hands.

What a terrific situation was it. Kunwar sahab's safety would have been vanished had there been a moment's delay. The lion's burning eyes were glaring in front of Basudha. Foul odour from its breathing touched her body. Her hands and feet were swollen. The intestines were shrinking within at the stink: yet the present terror, as though, filled electrifying strength in her nerves. She took control of her gun. Between herself and the lion was not even a two-hand long distance. It was about to come closer on tip-toe. When Basudha straightened the nozzle of the gun almost toward its eyes and fired. Boom! The lion's clutch at the platform loosened. It fell down.

The problem now was all the more dreadful. Kunwar sahab had fallen down within the reach of the lion's three-four steps. Maybe he had some grave injury also. If the lion was breathing still it must attack Kunwar sahab. Basudha's life was now centred inside her eyes, and her strength was centred in her wrists. At that moment if someone had hurled a lance into her body she would not have felt that. She was not in her senses. Her unconsciousness was working as consciousness. She switched an electric light and saw the lion was trying to get up on its feet. Promptly she fired her second shot on its head and then jumped down, with her revolver. The lion growled aloud. Basudha lept toward it, aimed her revolver near its mouth and emptied its magazine. By that time Kunwar sahab stood up pulling himself together. He ran toward her and clung her together holding fast to his bosom. Well! What was it!

Basudha was unconscious. The terror as though had held her life in its grip, thereby was protecting herself till her last shot. Soon as the terror subsided, she had fallen senseless.

7

About three hours later Basudha's unconsciousness came to its end. In her awareness, she was still thinking of that terror-stricken situation. Scared still, she opened her eyes slowly. Kunwar sahab asked: How are you feeling darling?

Basudha encircled him by both of her arms, as if in protection and replied: Move away from there. Or it might jump on you.

Kunwar sahab laughed: The lion is stilled now, quite long. It is there on the verandah. A lion of such stature and such terrible never have I seen before.

Basudha: You were not injured right?

Kunwar: Not at all. Why did you jump down. You might have been injured in your feet. It is strange how you could survive. From that height never could have jumped down.

Basudha asked amazingly: Me? When did I jump? The lion had come up to the platform, this I remember. What happened afterwards, I don't remember anything of that.

Kunwar became surprised: What a fun! You had fired at it twice. As it fell down, you too jumped down promptly, and pushed the nozzle of your revolver into its mouth. That's all, it became still. That was an undaunting animal. If you had missed then having fallen down, it would have attacked me forthwith. I did not have even a knife. The gun had slipped away from my hand and fallen on the opposite side. Nothing was visible in the darkness. I am standing here alive but for your grace. You have given me new life.

The very next day early in the morning the party beat a retreat.

8

The house that used to devour Basudha splitting her every moment, had so much pleasure for her as she returned, as though she was getting united with an estranged friend. It seemed every object there was welcoming her. The servants to whom she never spoke for months, today she asked all of them their welfare, with a smiling face and embraced them, as it were, she was veering her earlier rude treatment.

Upon the golden sea in the sky the twilight sun was navigating its boat. Settled comfortably in a chair facing a window Basudha was looking yonder at a sight. In that sight was, today, life, development and thrill. Even that abandoned hut of the boatman was looking so much pleasing. The nature was filled with charms.

In front of the temple Munia was making the Princes play. Overlooking them, by and by, Basudha felt surging devotion for the hereditary deity of the family; a feeling that remained subdued in her for years. She commanded that items for worshipping be brought to her, and then she went out to the temple to worship. Today she even could gift away things from her store-house filled in happiness. Out of her agonised heart that she had earlier, what else she could have been able to offer save the burning pain!

Right at that time Kunwar sahab came closer to her to ask: Are you going to the temple to worship? I too have sworn a pledge.

Basudha asked with smile in her eyes: What kind of a pledge?

Kunwar sahab replied with smiles: This I won't tell you.

❒❒❒